HEIDEGGER'S BEING

New Studies in Phenomenology and Hermeneutics

Kenneth Maly, General Editor

New Studies in Phenomenology and Hermeneutics aims to open up new approaches to classical issues in phenomenology and hermeneutics. Thus its intentions are the following: to further the work of Edmund Husserl, Maurice Merleau-Ponty, and Martin Heidegger – as well as that of Paul Ricoeur, Hans-Georg Gadamer, and Emmanuel Levinas; to enhance phenomenological thinking today by means of insightful interpretations of texts in phenomenology as they inform current issues in philosophical study; to inquire into the role of interpretation in phenomenological thinking: to take seriously Husserl's term phenomenology as "a science which is intended to supply the basic instrument for a rigorously scientific philosophy and, in its consequent application, to make possible a methodical reform of all the sciences"; to take up Heidegger's claim that "what is own to phenomenology, as a philosophical 'direction,' does not rest in being real. Higher than reality stands possibility. Understanding phenomenology consists solely in grasping it as possibility"; to practice phenomenology as "underway," as "the praxis of the self-showing of the matter for thinking," as "entering into the movement of enactment-thinking."

The commitment of this book series is also to provide English translations of significant works from other languages. In summary, **New Studies in Phenomenology and Hermeneutics** intends to provide a forum for a full and fresh thinking and rethinking of the way of phenomenology and interpretive phenomenology, that is, hermeneutics.

For a list of books published in the series, see page 189.

Heidegger's Being

The Shimmering Unfolding

RICHARD CAPOBIANCO

UNIVERSITY OF TORONTO PRESS
Toronto Buffalo London

© University of Toronto Press 2022
Toronto Buffalo London
utorontopress.com
Printed in the U.S.A.

ISBN 978-1-4875-4458-4 (cloth)
ISBN 978-1-4875-4643-4 (EPUB)
ISBN 978-1-4875-4644-1 (PDF)

New Studies in Phenomenology and Hermeneutics

Library and Archives Canada Cataloguing in Publication

Title: Heidegger's being : the shimmering unfolding / Richard Capobianco.
Other titles: Being : the shimmering unfolding | Shimmering unfolding
Names: Capobianco, Richard, 1957– author.
Series: New studies in phenomenology and hermeneutics (Toronto, Ont.)
Description: Series statement: New studies in phenomenology and
    hermeneutics | Includes bibliographical references and index.
Identifiers: Canadiana (print) 20210340037 | Canadiana (ebook)
    20210340045 | ISBN 9781487544584 (cloth) | ISBN 9781487546434 (EPUB) |
    ISBN 9781487546441 (PDF)
Subjects: LCSH: Heidegger, Martin, 1889–1976. | LCSH: Ontology. |
    LCSH: Philosophy, Modern – 20th century.
Classification: LCC B3279.H49 C365 2022 | DDC 193 – dc23

We wish to acknowledge the land on which the University of Toronto Press
operates. This land is the traditional territory of the Wendat, the Anishnaabeg,
the Haudenosaunee, the Métis, and the Mississaugas of the Credit First Nation.

University of Toronto Press acknowledges the financial support of the
Government of Canada, the Canada Council for the Arts, and the Ontario
Arts Council, an agency of the Government of Ontario, for its publishing
activities.

**Canada Council
for the Arts**   **Conseil des Arts
du Canada**

**ONTARIO ARTS COUNCIL
CONSEIL DES ARTS DE L'ONTARIO**
an Ontario government agency
un organisme du gouvernement de l'Ontario

Funded by the   Financé par le
Government   gouvernement
of Canada   du Canada

*Here after many hardships, endless wanderings, after twenty years,
I have come home at last.*

Odyssey, VI, 205

*Be not discouraged, keep on, there are divine things well envelop'd,
I swear to you there are divine things more beautiful than words can tell.*

Walt Whitman, from "Song of the Open Road"

Contents

Part III: Reflections and Impressions

HEIDEGGER'S BEING

Introduction

The beauty and resonance of the later Heidegger's thinking of
Being is the leitmotif of my two earlier books, *Engaging Heidegger*
and *Heidegger's Way of Being*. The present volume, the third in this
trilogy, brings together essays, a translation, and "reflections and
impressions" to amplify this leitmotif in new and fresh ways, but
also to draw out more vividly how the later Heidegger's thinking of Being ushers us close to ultimate "mystery."

Part I presents studies that offer rigorous textual elucidations
of a number of Heidegger's writings that have not received sufficient attention in the scholarship. Included here are studies on
Heidegger's commentary on Pindar's "gold" and Heraclitus's
kosmos (with a reference to a painting by the American artist
Andrew Wyeth) (Chapter 1); Heidegger's "turn" (*die Kehre*) in
thinking to Being as *physis* and *aletheia* as documented in selected
published volumes of the *Black Notebooks* (Chapter 2); the full
sweep of his "manifold thinking" of Being (Chapter 3, in tribute
to the late Prof. William J. Richardson); his concerted effort to
overcome the "egoity" (*Ichheit*) of our contemporary age (Chapter 4); the implications of his thinking on *mythos* and Being for
the appropriation of a religious tradition (Chapter 5); and his
1940s lecture courses on Heraclitus and the intriguing hints
therein of a "process metaphysics" of some fashion (Chapter 6).
The final chapter in Part I (Chapter 7) is an extensive dialogue
with Prof. Vladimír Leško of Slovakia that charts my own path
through Heidegger's thinking, while also bringing into sharper

relief Heidegger's central notions and his life-long consideration of Parmenides and Heraclitus, Plato and Aristotle.[1]

Part II offers a translation of a delightful address given by the Japanese scholar Kōichi Tsujimura on the occasion of Heidegger's 80th birthday celebration in 1969. His talk is in accord with a guiding theme of this volume that Heidegger's thought unfolds a certain "spiritual" comportment toward all things, and Tsujimura attests to what he understands to be the close connection between Heidegger's fundamental outlook and the ancient Zen Buddhist wisdom as exemplified by several Zen masters, including Dōgen. In addition, Heidegger's brief "Reply in Appreciation" affords us an insight into how in the later work he came to understand Being as "the Nothing" (*das Nichts*) in a more existentially "whole" and "wholesome" manner than in the early writings. That is, for the later Heidegger, "the Nothing" is no longer anything "negative" at all, but rather the overflowing fullness from out of which all things arise, including ourselves.

In Part III, I offer a series of reflections and impressions that take their inspiration, in part, from Heidegger's own engaging entries in his *Black Notebooks*. Each note in Part III makes a point but at the same time invites further consideration. I would like to think that these notes offer a short-form style of philosophical reflection that are pedagogically useful insofar as they give rise to one good insight or one good question. Several notes seek primarily to clarify and elucidate, while others trace parallels with other thinkers and poets, such as Alfred North Whitehead, C.G. Jung, Robert Frost, Walt Whitman, and even the Persian poet Rumi; and some other notes offer a particular text that crystallizes in a striking way a central theme of Heidegger's thinking. Despite the variety of topics, the reader will be able to discern the common thread that runs through all these reflections.

Thus the three parts of this book, taken together, offer an earnest effort on my part to convey once again the extraordinary reach and richness of Heidegger's thinking. The book is intended not only for dedicated students of Heidegger's work but also for all those who wish to come to a deeper appreciation of his distinctive understanding of Being and its implications. Above all,

I invite readers along a path of meditative thinking – a path that is, alas, rarely taken these days, even in philosophy.

I am aware that some readers will be surprised or puzzled by the suggestions in these pages that the later Heidegger's reflections often leaned in the direction of a refashioned "metaphysical" outlook; but as I see it, the texts themselves tell the tale, and I am hopeful that readers will join me in attending closely to what they have to say. Moreover, I gently remind readers that genuine thinking, by whatever name, is inevitably led to consider, in one way or another, all things and ultimate matters. Heidegger's vision of Being was, in the end, simply too far-reaching and all-embracing to be limited to the sphere of the human. We are part of the story, to be sure, but not the whole story of what he poetically described – inspired especially by Heraclitus's sayings – as this "shimmering *kosmos*."

PART I

Studies

1 Pindar's "Gold" and Heraclitus's "*Kosmos*" as Being Itself

Beauty belongs to the unfolding of Being.

Heidegger (GA 73.1: 134)

Kosmos [as *physis*] shimmers ungraspably through everything.

Heidegger (GA 15: 282)

The shining star in the night sky is beautiful. Yet what always struck Heidegger as even more beautiful was the "hidden" motion – the way – wherein and whereby the star comes to shine so brightly. This "way" he named Being in distinction from beings (the "ontological difference"), and, as he saw it, Being was named *kosmos* by Heraclitus. In my earlier books *Engaging Heidegger* and *Heidegger's Way of Being*, I have elucidated how Heidegger understood the earliest Greek thinkers to have caught sight of the Being-way and named it as *physis*, *aletheia*, and the primordial *Logos*. Yet only in passing have I addressed his reflections on *kosmos* as an early Greek name for Being itself, and the contemporary scholarship has altogether missed the significant role that this Greek *Ur*-word plays in his later thinking. The "shimmering," "gleaming," "adorning" *kosmos* – which the later Heidegger understood to be "world" (*Welt*) in the fullest and richest sense – is not in the first place any kind of projection of the human being or of the gods; rather, it is the resplendence of the Being-unfolding-way from out of which both the gods and human beings issue forth and come to pass.

I. Pindar's "Gold" Names Being Itself

On 9 September 1966, in Le Thor, Heidegger highlighted for his French colleagues his reading of Heraclitus's understanding of *kosmos* (GA 15).[1] Not long after this meeting, he engaged the matter again in the joint seminar with Eugen Fink in the winter semester 1966–7 at Freiburg (GA 15). The dialogue with Fink, as interesting as it is, is a more difficult source to draw upon because it is often not clear what precisely Heidegger's position is in relation to Fink's. In any case, all of his statements on Heraclitus's *kosmos* made in the 1950s and 1960s rest principally upon his detailed and lengthy reading of fragment 30 in his lecture course on Heraclitus given at Freiburg during the summer semester of 1943. Although he discussed fragment 30 in reflections prior to 1943, we may consider the 1943 lecture course to be his principal reading of *kosmos*.

In *Heidegger's Way of Being*, two chapters are devoted to his brilliantly creative readings of Heraclitus's fragments in the lecture courses in 1943 and 1944, which were collected in GA 55, published in 1979, and only recently translated into English. In the chapter titled "Sentinels of Being," I made note of his reading of *kosmos*, but here I would like to develop his line of thinking more completely and draw out the implications more fully.[2]

Yet to accomplish this, we must take a step back to a lecture course on the saying of Anaximander that he had prepared in 1942 but did not deliver. The text of the lecture course was recently published as GA 78, and the reading that he unfolds is as compelling as the readings of Parmenides and Heraclitus that he undertook in this same extraordinarily creative period of the early 1940s. In this lecture course text, he also engaged in a lengthy discursus on several lines from Pindar's *Isthmian Ode 5*, and his commentary is especially important for our purposes. To crystallize his elucidation: After carefully laying out the ancient Greek experience of Being as temporal shining forth, he turns to the opening lines (verses 1–18) of Pindar's *Ode*. Heidegger is especially concerned with the first three lines, which in English translation are usually rendered:

Mother of the Sun, Theia of many names,
Because of you men value gold (*chryson*) as mighty
above all other things (*periosion allon*)[3]

He focuses on Pindar's words *periosion allon*, and he notes that these words are said in relation to "gold" (*chryson*, 67). His effort is to clarify this relation.

He observes that *periosion* is the Ionian form of the word *periousios* (60), and this tells us that Pindar's word speaks to *peri* and *ousia* – the "around" (*peri*) "what-comes-to-presence" (*ousia*). For Heidegger, *periosion allon* in this line speaks not simply to what shines forth (beings and beings as a whole) but moreover to the shining or gleaming or glowing that *allows* everything (*allon*) to shine forth in the first place. What is principally brought into view is the unique radiance or gleam (*Glanz, glänzen*) that allows every particular being, as well as the whole ensemble of beings, to shine forth in the first place. How, then, is this unique primordial gleam named by Pindar? The word in the *Ode* is "gold," which is esteemed by human beings above "everything" else. Thus, as Heidegger reads the lines, Pindar had caught sight of and composed a hymn to that which allows all beings to be – and this is Being itself. Pindar glimpsed the very essencing of Being as "gold," as that which "gleams about or around" (*umglänzt*) all beings. The originary Greek experience of Being was brought to language in this poetizing: "Pindar's song thinks Being in the name of gold" (94).[4] Being is named in the Greek word *einai*, Heidegger tells us, and Pindar's word "gold" is precisely "this illuminating and illuminating-about-and-around illumination [that] gives us the hint into *einai*" (295). The human being "glimpses" Being itself as "gold," but he warns that this must not be construed in a manner that would bring Being under the yoke of the human being. The "lighting-clearing itself" is *not* the human being:

> From out of this essence of the human being we first experience wherein the Greek of the "Greek human being" lies. "The Greek human being" does not provide the measure for the understanding of "Being," but rather it is the manner in which "Being" is cleared as *einai* that determines the essence of the human being. The lighting-clearing itself [*die Lichtung selbst*] calls to the human being in the dispensation of its essence.   (295)

II. Heraclitus's *Kosmos* Is Being Itself

With all this in mind, we turn to his elucidation of fragment 30 in the 1943 lecture course (GA 55). His reading is related to his elucidations of the other fragments of Heraclitus, and already in the lecture course he had clarified that "fire" (*pur*) is to be understood as that which allows all beings to flame up in the first place and that the "lightning flash" (*keraunos*) is that which "steers" all beings into their proper place. The "fire" and "lightning flash" of Heraclitus's sayings are names for the pure emerging that is *physis*, which in turn is a name for Being itself. According to Heidegger, Heraclitus is always drawing our attention to that which *enables* all beings to be as they are, and as they are in relation to one another in the ensemble. Being itself as *physis* as "ever-living fire" as "lightning flash" is this pure temporal emerging-manifesting way that has gone overlooked in the history of metaphysical thinking. Yet Heraclitus also named this "way" as *kosmos*.

Heidegger's remarks on fragment 30 in the lecture course are dense and difficult to decipher, and no doubt this is one reason that the significance of his elucidation of *kosmos* has been largely passed over or missed. His play with the language is artful but also obscure; nevertheless, his fundamental point is clear enough, and that is what I wish to focus upon. He tells us once again that what Heraclitus was seeking to bring into view in the sayings was *physis* as the pure "emerging" that "opens up" all beings in the first place: *physis* as "the inapparent joining, the noble opening up, the from-out-of-itself essencing lighting-clearing" (163). It is from out of *physis*, this "lighting-clearing joining," that "appears and shines forth beings as a whole."

This shining-joining, he continues, that allows all beings to shine forth and steers them together in the ensemble is named in the German language with the words *das Schmücken* and *das Zieren*. These are two words often mentioned and favored by Heidegger but, again, often overlooked by commentators. The two words are very close in meaning, and in English, we have a variety of words that we may employ to translate: emblazoning, adorning, embellishing, decorating, bedecking, decking out, festooning, gracing. It is best that we keep all of these English words in play as we follow Heidegger's discussion because his key point is that *das Schmücken* and *das Zieren*, this emblazoning and adorning, does not in the first place refer to any particular being or thing that shines forth brilliantly, but rather to "the lighting-clearing letting-appear" itself (*das lichtende Erscheinenlassen*) by which and through which everything is steered to its proper place and radiates and gleams from itself. *Physis* is this "primordial emblazoning and adorning" (*das ursprüngliche Schmücken und Zieren*), but this is also the fundamental meaning of the Greek word *kosmos* as employed by Heraclitus: "*kosmos ist die Zier*" (163), Heidegger states. *Kosmos* is another name for the primordial emblazoning-adorning – this shimmering *kosmos* – and both words, *kosmos* and *die Zier*, also convey the sense of what "stands out" and is "noble" and full of "honor" (*Ehre, Auszeichnung*). Accordingly, the highest god Zeus bore the name *kosmos*, and the Cretans called their political leaders *kosmoi*; but more fundamentally, the sense is of all beings – everything – "appearing in the light, standing in the open of renown and radiance" (164).[5]

In naming *kosmos*, therefore, Heraclitus was naming the genuine to-be-thought (*das Zu-denkende*), and the to-be-thought is not simply beings, or even beings as a whole, but that which enables all beings to be, namely, Being itself. As Heidegger clearly and explicitly puts it: "*die 'Zier' – kosmos – is* then indeed to be said of Being itself" (164). He cautions that we must not read back into Heraclitus's *Ur*-word our modern understanding of "cosmos" and "cosmology," for these terms can do no better than refer to beings as a whole. Rather, we must understand *kosmos* from out of "the oneness of essence (*Wesenseinheit*) with *physis*, *harmonia*, and *me dunon pote*," and this means thinking *kosmos* as the emblazoning-adorning that lets beings, and beings as a whole, flare up and gleam in the first place. In this sense, then, *kosmos* as *die Zier* is precisely "the lightning flash" (*der Blitz*) and "the fire" (*das Feuer*) spoken of by Heraclitus in several other fragments. *Kosmos* is as *die Zier* the "dispensing" or "sending" (*schickende*) of beings-along-their-way and as such:

> This emblazoning-adorning thus thought as [the] lighting-clearing joining, [that is, as] *physis*, *zoe*, *harmonia*, is the emblazoning-adorning fire itself, the lightning flash. *Kosmos* and fire say the Same. (164)

Only with these considerations in mind, he maintains, can we approach in a truly thoughtful way fragment 30, in which we find the key word *aeizoon*, the "ever-living":

> *kosmon ton auton hapanton oute tis theon oute anthropon epoiesen, all' en aei kai estin kai estai pur aeizoon, haptomenon metra kai aposbennumenon metra.*

Fragment 30 is typically translated into English along the lines of:

> This world, which is the same for all, no one of gods or humans has made; but it was ever, is now, and ever shall be an ever-living fire, with measures kindling and measures going out.

We will return to Heidegger's own translation of the fragment, but it is more helpful to attend first to his commentary. He notes that the fragment speaks to *kosmos* as *die Zier* as the joining and ordering of all beings as a whole. All beings are the emblazoned and adorned in the ordered ensemble, and this ensemble he refers to, using the Greek phrase, the "apparent harmony" (*harmonia phanere*). Yet in his view, Heraclitus's chief concern was with the "inapparent harmony" (*harmonia aphanes*), that is, the "hidden" joining and ordering motion through and throughout all beings.

This fundamental "difference" (*Unterschied*) between the "inapparent harmony" (*kosmos*) and the "apparent harmony" of all beings is brought to light by the fragment, according to Heidegger, and we hear in his characterization of the matter an echo of his life-long concern with the "ontological difference," or simply the "difference," between Being and beings. It is this "difference," he further explains, that enables us to understand Heraclitus's fragment 124 as well. According to this saying, an arrangement of beings is truly beautiful only because of the inapparent unitary joining-ordering that is *kosmos* itself (163). In other words, for Heidegger, as he reads Heraclitus, *kosmos* (as Being itself) is always prior in "beauty" and importance to beings and to their beautiful array in the ensemble.

III.   The Primacy of Being Itself as *Kosmos*

It is precisely the priority and primacy of Being itself that Heidegger understands to be highlighted in fragment 30. He notes that the singular emblazoning-adorning (*die Zier*), and therefore *kosmos*, is lost from view when the focus is on beings in their resplendence. This focus on beings, he suggests, also moves the human being (or the gods) to the center of attention at the expense of the primordial emblazoning-adorning. Yet, in the saying, Heraclitus is explicit and emphatic that the primordial emblazoning-adorning is "not made or produced, neither by one of the gods nor by one of the human beings," and he adds, "*physis* is beyond the gods and human beings" (166). What is more:

> Every metaphysical kind of consideration, whether it proceeds with God as the first cause or with the human being as the center of all objectifying, fails if it should attempt to think what is given to be thought in this saying [of Heraclitus]. *Prior to every being and*

> *prior to every origination of a being from a being, Being itself essences*
> *[west].* It *[Being itself] is nothing made and has therefore also no deter-*
> *minate beginning at a point in time and no corresponding ending of its*
> *existence.*   (166, italics mine)

There are several important points to be considered. Heidegger proposes that Heraclitus's *kosmos* as Being itself is altogether missed not only by the kind of traditional metaphysical
thinking that posits a divine being as the first cause but also by
the kind of modern transcendental-phenomenological thinking that posits the human knower as the center of all objectifying. Thus we hear in the first line a critique of the thinking of
Descartes-Kant-Husserl as much as a critique of the thinking
of Plato-Aristotle-Aquinas. Furthermore, the priority and primacy of Being itself in relation to all beings is made perfectly
clear in the second sentence. Being itself is not a being; Being
itself is the temporal way wherein and whereby all beings come
to pass and, as such, is prior in importance and more luminous and beautiful than any particular being or than beings as
a whole.

Since Being itself is prior to every being, it is therefore
prior to the human being. At the very least, this priority is
structural; that is, in the correlation of Being and the human
being, Being precedes and exceeds the human being and is in
no way reducible to what is posited or constituted in "meaning" by the human being. In other words, then, Being is not
dependent upon the human being (or the gods). Heidegger
takes very much to heart that Heraclitus says in fragment 30
that Being as *kosmos* is the "ever-living fire" that "always was,
is, and always will be." Thus Being as *kosmos* is the temporal ever-unfolding of beings that is not dependent upon the
human being – or to say the same thing – Being is *independent*
of the human being.

Being is not any kind of timeless onto-theological supreme
entity or first cause or first principle, but it is *also* not that which
is correlated with the human being in such a way that it is dependent upon the human being. This passage certainly suggests that

Being "is" (or "essences" or "unfolds") even if the human being is not, and – let us be clear – this means that his position is simply incompatible with Husserl's or with any strict transcendental-phenomenological approach. A text such as this one, unfortunately overlooked in the scholarship, attests to the effect of the "turn" in Heidegger's thinking after the 1920s and makes evident that the later Heidegger's thinking of Being is at a great distance from the "transcendental idealism" of his teacher, Husserl, and from any other "transcendental" philosophical perspectives that would hold that there is "Being" only insofar as there is the human being.

IV. *Kosmos* as Being Itself Is "Measure" for All Beings

Heidegger once more offers a cautionary note that Heraclitus's thinking on *kosmos* (as Being itself) is not addressed and appreciated in the understanding of "cosmos" in the natural sciences (166–7). For now, we can let his observation stand, but, in fact, there may be good reason to think that the richest reflections in contemporary theoretical astrophysics do indeed dovetail, or at least touch upon, what Heidegger was seeking after in elucidating the Heraclitean *kosmos* as Being itself. Even so, this is a discussion for another time.

There is in the lecture course text at this point (167–8) a parenthetical remark wherein he seeks to clarify the "temporal" character of the "eternal" *kosmos*. For Heidegger, "eternity" does not mean without time, but clarifying the proper character of the "time" of "eternity," that is, the primordial "time" proper to *kosmos*, is a difficult matter, which he only raises as an issue in the paragraph. He proceeds with the elucidation of fragment 30 with a kind of summary statement that "the unfolding emblazoning-adorning (*die Zier*) that is prior to all that is makeable and producible, in whose radiance gleams the lighting-clearing (*die Lichtung*) of everything illuminated-cleared, is *pur aeizoon*, the ever-emerging fire" (168). In his view, enough has been said to show how *kosmos* is the primordial emblazoning-adorning as "ever-living" and "ever-emerging" "fire" and how, therefore, *kosmos* is another name for *physis* and *harmonia* – and for Being itself. There remains to elucidate the last part of the fragment, which reads:

pur aeizoon, haptomenon metra kai aposbennumenon metra.

Usual English translation: "an ever-living fire, with measures kindling and measures going out."

Heidegger's translation: "*Feuer immerdar aufgehend, entzündend sich die Weiten, sich verlöschend die Weiten.*"   (168)

My translation of Heidegger's: "fire ever-emerging, expanses kindling themselves, expanses extinguishing themselves."

In this part of Heraclitus's saying, Heidegger finds a difficulty with the translation of the Greek word *metra* or *metron*. He notes that *pur* (fire) is named together with *metron*, and therefore "fire" (as *physis*) and *metron* are thought together. *Metron* is therefore in "essence" related to *physis*, *harmonia*, and *kosmos*, and he inquires into the proper translation of *metron*. "Measure" (*Maß*) is a "correct" translation, he observes, but he is wary of this word "measure" because it is has come to mean something very different in the modern mathematical thinking of the natural sciences. For the natural sciences, it is perfectly evident how fire alternately blazes up and is extinguished; this happens "according to measures," which means according to certain "laws of nature" that are comprehensible in exact mathematical terms. This modern scientific understanding of "according to measures" is an obstacle to a proper understanding of Heraclitus's saying, yet it has become so dominant and unquestioned that it compromises the translations of the fragment by philologists such as Diels-Kranz and Snell, both of whom translate the word *metra* (*metron*) in the fragment with "*nach Maßen*," "according to measures" (169).

The modern scientific understanding of *kosmos* as "fire" igniting and extinguishing "according to measures" will not do, but neither will any "theologically metaphysical cosmological" attestation be helpful. Simply having recourse to the "Old

Testatment" will not suffice, he observes; the real challenge is to make a concerted effort to understand Heraclitus's words in a truly Greek manner (170). As he reads the Greek, *haptomenon* means more precisely to "alight" in the sense of "making light, letting become bright, lighting, opening up the light." This gets us a step closer toward understanding what *metron* means in the saying. *To metron* does indeed mean "measure" in the sense of a measurement of weight or length, but this is not the primary or primordial sense of the word. A measuring stick can "measure" only because space has been "measured out" or opened out in the first place, so, for Heidegger, the fundamental meaning (*die Grundbedeutung*) of "measure" is as "dimension," "expanse," "the open." When the Greeks spoke of *metron thalasses*, they did not mean a measurement of the sea, but rather "the expanse of the sea" or "the open sea" (170). Accordingly, we are now able to catch sight of what Heraclitus was seeing and saying: *physis-kosmos-pur-*(fire)-*die Zier* (as the primordial emblazoning-adorning) *is* the primordial measuring out that is the lighting-clearing (*die Lichtung*), the expanse (*die Weite*), the open (*das Offene*), in which and by which all beings and things shine forth. Yet we must not forget that *physis* as "the ever-emerging fire" is "self-concealing" and "self-closing" as well; there is always borne along the dimension of reserve and sheltering. It is thus that, according to the fragment, "the ever-emerging fire" endlessly kindles *and extinguishes*, lightens *and darkens*.

Only by virtue of *kosmos* as *die Zier* as the Open can all beings – including human beings – be at all. Thus Heidegger concludes his remarks in this section by affirming once more that in no way does fragment 30 say that the primordial "fire" as *kosmos* as *physis* unfolds itself "according to" measure; rather, *physis is* the measure of all; it is "the measure-giving":

The ever-emerging fire directs itself not in the first place "according to" measures, but rather gives the measures in the properly understood sense of *metron*. The primordial emblazoning-adorning (*Zier*), *kosmos*, is the measure-giving; the measure that *kosmos* gives is it itself as *physis*. (171)

V. *Kosmos* in Later Writings

As I mentioned at the outset, Heidegger and Fink discussed at some length fragment 30 in their joint seminar in 1966–7 (GA 15). Some of the basic elements of Heidegger's 1943 reading are clearly discernible in their exchange, but one probably learns more about Fink's position than Heidegger's. A more direct and personal later reference to *kosmos* may be found in *Sojourns*, the philosophical journal or travelogue that he composed at the time of his first visit to Greece in 1962. Upon their ship reaching the island of Rhodes, "the island of roses," and "as the blue of the sky and the sea changed by the hour," he meditated on the "dark fire" brought to the Greeks from the East and how it inspired Greek thought and poetry (229). It was along this way that Heraclitus came to think the flaring up of all that is present as *kosmos* as *der Schmuck* and *die Zier*, the emblazoning-adorning, which was not created or made by the gods or humans (229). More precisely, *kosmos* as *die Zier* names "the illuminating, that which brings something to shine forth"; it names "the ever-emerging fire," which, according to fragment 30, endlessly measures out all things. With reflections such as these, Heidegger tells us in his travel journal, he passed the day "in conversation with Heraclitus."

In 1966, he reprised his reading of fragment 30, this time with French colleagues and friends in a seminar in Le Thor on 9 September at the house of the poet René Char (GA 15). Heidegger begins with a full translation of the saying that calls to mind his 1943 reading:

> This *kosmos* here, insofar as it is the same for all and for all that is, none of the gods, as well as no one of the human beings, has brought it forth, [for] it always already was and it is and will be: inexhaustibly living fire kindling itself in measures, extinguishing in measures.   (280)

The reading that follows is a highly condensed version of his 1943 reading, but several of his comments deserve additional consideration. He states that fragment 30 speaks to the "eternity" of the Heraclitean *kosmos*, and, as he had in the earlier reading, he observes that this eternity must be thought in terms of time: "eternity does not prevail over time" (281). What the saying points to is that "this world here has not been made, since it was already there at all times" and that "it is simply said [in the fragment] that as far back as one may go, *this* 'world' was already there." Therefore, he affirms once more the priority and independence of *kosmos*/world in relation to human beings (and the gods).

In this reading, Heidegger specifically calls attention to his use of the word "world" (*Welt*) in speaking of the Heraclitean *kosmos*, and this is significant. He is, as always, careful to distinguish the Heraclitean world/*kosmos* from modern conceptions of "world" as a great space or container for all other beings. The Heraclitean world/*kosmos* is rather "a way of being" (*eine Weise zu sein*), and he proceeds to elucidate *kosmos* in terms of die Zier and der Schmuck and "gold" (281–2) – all of which we have already discussed. Yet what needs to be highlighted here is that, for Heidegger, "world" is primarily and primordially the Heraclitean *kosmos* (as Being itself) and *not* that which is projected by the human being and thereby dependent upon the human being. The Greek word *kosmos* as used by Heraclitus manifests "the fundamental relation of the Greek language to nature (*Natur*)," which "consists in letting nature itself open in its radiance." For this reason, he adds, the Greek language "names the *kosmos* as older (*älter*) than gods and human beings, who remain related back to it [*kosmos*], since no one of them could ever have brought it forth" (282). We must appreciate the full import of Heidegger's statement: *kosmos*/world/Nature is "older" than the gods and human beings; in other words, the essencing or unfolding of *kosmos*/world/Nature (and therefore of Being itself) is not dependent upon the gods or upon human beings.

Concluding Thought

A few years ago, the National Gallery of Art in Washington, DC, mounted a major exhibition of a number of paintings by the American artist Andrew Wyeth, and the centerpiece of the show was Wyeth's 1947 painting *Wind from the Sea*.[6] The image is simple enough: an open window through which we see a field of dry grass and two dirt tracks that lead to the shore. Beyond the open field, there are clusters of dark woods and above the woods a big, blank sky. Yet on the interior side of the window, there is a sudden motion that breaks the stillness of the composed elements. The nearly transparent lace curtains hanging at the window billow out gently; a wind has caught them and lifted them up and out into the room. It is this surprising, spontaneous motion that captivates. All at once, we realize that everything in the image – the window, the grass, the water, the woods, the sky – is not static and still, but in motion. Everything is being moved along by this hidden breath of air.

Wyeth, we may say, captured in an image what Heidegger brought to language and what he understood Heraclitus to have brought to language: the "hidden harmony" (*harmonia aphanes*) that moves all beings along their way and "shimmers ungraspably through everything." Being itself as *physis* as *kosmos*. The unfolding – the way – of all beings, which is not a being itself but the Being-way of all beings, is indeed manifest – yet only indirectly and glancingly. The Being-way cannot be "seen" in any usual way, and for this reason, it is "inapparent" or "hidden"; but it "gleams" nonetheless for those who are open and receptive and accepting: in the billowing of a curtain; in the low murmur of a propeller plane making its way across the soft summer sky; in the puff of white snow drifting off the branches of a pine tree on a cold, perfectly still winter's day; in the luminous moon suddenly emerging from behind thick clouds in the harvest-time night sky. Heidegger caught sight of what artists and poets have seen all along, and he brought it into a poetic philosophical language that is compelling and distinctive. It is all too easy to lament the difficulty and obscurity of some of Heidegger's language in his reflections on the Being-way, but the challenge – and reward – is to come to see in his saying *die Sache selbst*, the core matter itself – and then to say it again for ourselves.

2 In the *Black Notebooks*: The "Turn" Away from the Transcendental-Phenomenological Positioning of *Being and Time* to the Thinking of Being as *Physis* and *Aletheia*

Philosophy is never "of" or "about" something – always only for – for Being.

Heidegger, *Black Notebooks*, 1931

Heidegger's *Black Notebooks* have already generated a cottage industry of commentary, too much of which has been no more than "reaction" – and overreaction – to a handful of entries among hundreds and hundreds in the four thick volumes published thus far. Even if one agrees that a considered vetting of some of the more callous and inflammatory entries is necessary and appropriate, still, there is much more to these notebooks that deserve attention, and particularly his properly philosophical notes that are helpful in elucidating his principal ideas and terms and in clarifying the development of his thinking. It will take time and patience to sort out the philosophical import of all these reflections, and it would do well for us to keep this in mind as the remaining notebooks from the 1950s and later years are brought to publication. In the long run, however, these notebooks will be chiefly of interest to Heidegger scholars and not essential reading for an understanding of Heidegger's central ideas and themes. What is more, no matter how strenuous the effort made by some recently, the distinction between Heidegger the man and his times and Heidegger the thinker cannot be collapsed. The work of every great philosopher, poet, artist, composer – the creative work of any person – can never be reduced to biography.

I.   The "Leap" to the Thinking of Being Itself (GA 94)

To maintain a sharp focus, let us consider a small selection of entries from the first volume (GA 94) and the fourth volume (GA 97) of the notebooks that have been published.[1] These particular entries offer us additional guidance on Heidegger's "turn" (*die Kehre*) after *Being and Time* and on his later thinking of Being as *physis* and *aletheia*. In GA 94, which covers the years 1931–8, there are two remarkably revealing entries (*Überlegungen*, "considerations"). The first brings into view in an especially striking manner his transition from *Being and Time*:

> *Being and Time* is not a "philosophy about time," and even less so a teaching on the "temporality" (*Zeitlichkeit*) of the human being, but rather clearly and surely *a* path to the grounding of the truth of Being; of *Being itself*, and not of beings, and also not of beings *as* beings. Leading the way is the leap into "Temporality" (*Temporalität*), into that wherein primordial time with primordial space essence together *as* unfoldings of the essencing of truth, of its [truth's] transporting-transfixing clearing (*Lichtung*) and concealing. Of course, [therefore], the first, insufficient version of the third section of the first part of *Being and Time* had to be destroyed.
>
> (GA 94: 272; Heidegger's italics)

One may say that the entirety of the "turn" in Heidegger's thinking is crystallized in this single entry. Reading GA 94, one is struck by how dissatisfied Heidegger had become not only with the reception and appraisal of *Being and Time* by contemporary readers, but also with his own approach. In an indirect manner, he appears to admit that his thinking in *Being and Time* was still too colored by a transcendental approach and its terminology. In a related entry, he allows that his seeking after the "understanding of Being" (*Seinsverständnis*) in *Being and Time* posed the core matter in an insufficient way, for it presented the "danger" of construing

Being and Time as proffering only another "idealism" (GA 94: 248–9). Although he is insistent throughout that this is a misreading of the posing and unfolding of the Being-question in *Being and Time*, he is nonetheless aware of the difficulties and limitations of his own *Daseinsanalytik*. Thus in the full entry cited above, he makes it clear that in *Being and Time* he was not principally concerned with proceeding in a transcendental manner in uncovering the "temporality of the human being." Rather, all along, and in *Being and Time* in particular, his aim was to attain to a thinking of the "temporality" of "Being itself." Yet this is precisely what the transcendental positioning in *Being and Time* prevented him from achieving, and we hear his frustration and even exasperation as he reports, rather dramatically, that his effort to finish *Being and Time* had to be "destroyed." The task for thinking that he had proposed simply could not be accomplished by continuing within the Neo-Kantian and Husserlian transcendental framework.

What, then, was needed for (his) thinking? The entry tells us: a "leap" out of the transcendental approach. But a "leap" out of transcendental-phenomenology to – what kind of thinking? We could say that this is precisely what Heidegger attempted to answer for himself over the remaining nearly fifty years of his lifetime of thinking and writing. Even so, what he does make evident here, if we read carefully enough, is that with this "leap," the transcendental framing of *Being and Time* had to be abandoned and left for ruins. The Being-question survives, but little else. Indeed, there should be no surprise or puzzlement among commentators that so many of the thematic elements of *Being and Time* – such as the tool analysis – vanish in Heidegger's later thinking. The "leap" left these transcendental-phenomenological micro-analyses behind once and for all.

Yet, again, a leap whereunto? He offers a sketch of where (his) thinking must go, and we recognize in the dense sentence of the entry several of the key features of his later thought. Thus thinking must make a "leap" over the transcendental analysis of Dasein's *Zeitlichkeit* in *Being and Time* to the *Temporalität* of Being itself. To think the "temporality" of Being itself means bringing to language "primordial time" and "primordial space" as they "essence" or unfold together. In the later thinking, this is the leitmotif of the "time-(play)-space" (the *Zeit-Raum* and *Zeit-Spiel-Raum*) of Being itself. It was the "time-space" of Being that was sought after in *Being and Time* but which could never be attained by remaining within the transcendental paradigm. Only with a "leap" in thinking can we arrive at the fundamental temporalizing-spatializing of Being itself, which is the (groundless) ground of the human being's own temporal-spatial existence.

There are other prefigurings as well. We also hear the later theme of Being itself unfolding as "truth." "Truth" does not in the first place belong to the human being, but rather to the "essencing" or "unfolding" (self-showing, emerging, shining forth) of Being itself. Furthermore, the "truth" of Being itself is named here by Heidegger as the "clearing" (*Lichtung*) that reveals-conceals, and this brings into view his key later position that "the clearing itself is Being," as he put it so emphatically in *Letter on Humanism* (1947).[2] In this one entry, then, we learn where the "leap" in thinking must go: (1) to the "temporality" and "time-space" of Being itself (and not simply of the human being); (2) to the "truth" of Being itself (and not simply "truth" as the disclosive activity of the human being); and (3) to the clearing itself as Being itself (and not simply as the clearing activity of the human being). This one entry captures Heidegger's deep dissatisfaction and struggle with his own *Daseinsanalytik* in *Being and Time* – and how he set for himself the task of making a "leap" beyond it to fulfill the promise of the *Seinsfrage*.

The second "consideration" from GA 94 is related to the first and is also especially instructive:

> *The fundamental experience of my thinking*: The predominancy of Beyng before all beings … Beyng, however, not as object of thinking and representing, and the predominancy [of Beyng] not as the a priori in the sense of the condition of objectifying; all of this is only the foreground and distant consequence of the primal inceptualizing – but again rapidly receding – Beyng. The predominancy of Beyng [as] unfolding in the primordial truth – from out of which [primordial truth], and in which therefrom, every being arises in the first place.
>
> (GA 94: 362; Heidegger's italics)

This entry reveals Heidegger's need to affirm that no matter the confusions in his own earlier work and especially in *Being and Time*, and no matter the confusions in the critical responses to *Being and Time*, one thing was certain: the fundamental experience of his thinking from the outset was the "predominancy of Beyng before all beings." It is apparent that he did not have this clarity about his project when he composed *Being and Time*, and for this reason *Being and Time* could not and did not work out the *primacy of Being* in a direct and decisive manner. The *Daseinsanalytik* fell short of the professed aim of the *Seinsfrage*.

The entry also speaks to his clarity regarding the limitation of the transcendental approach to Being. He alludes to the fact that in all transcendental approaches, Being is reduced to either (1) the object of thinking and representing or (2) the full array of the cognitive conditions of the possibility for any object (of thinking and representing) coming before us. He rejects both reductions as inadequate, as mere "foreground" and "distant" from the fundamental matter. The transcendental-phenomenological "a priori" can never attain to the ontological priority of "Beyng before all beings." What is needed, therefore, is a more fundamental thinking that makes manifest how the human being and its noetic activity – no matter how deconstructed and broadly understood – is ontologically "grounded" or "founded" in the first place. Consequently, certain leading themes of all his later work thereby take shape in this entry: Being as "primal inceptualizing" (Being as *Ereignis* and as *Es gibt*) and Being as "primordial truth" (*physis* and *aletheia*) as the temporal-spatial unfolding/emerging/ opening/clearing of all beings, including the human being.

Thus, patiently considered, these two entries in GA 94 give us a clearer and fuller picture of Heidegger's abandonment of the transcendental-phenomenological positioning that still marked *Being and Time* and of his decisive "turn" to the thinking of Being itself.

II. Being Itself as *Physis* and *Aletheia* (GA 97)

Let us move our attention to GA 97, the fourth published volume of the notebooks covering the years 1942–8, because here we find the "later" Heidegger fully underway. These "observations"

(*Anmerkungen*) parallel, in part, his creative readings of Parmenides, Heraclitus, and Anaximander of the 1940s, in which he unfolded his understanding of Being as *physis, aletheia*, and the primordial *Logos*. There can be no understanding of the later Heidegger's thinking of Being without an understanding of his readings of the earliest Greek thinkers, so it is important to consider how these readings are reflected in the notebooks. In particular, his understanding of Being as "primordial truth" is now fully developed in these notebooks from the 1940s.

One of Heidegger's most original and distinctive positions is that Being "is" "primordial truth" or "*aletheia*." Yet it is precisely this position that appears to generate the most resistance in some recent readings of his work. Why? Principally because it refuses the modern transcendental and analytic position that the human being is the sole "locus" of truth. Heidegger struggled to find his own voice on the matter of "truth" throughout the 1920s, and this is evident in the ambiguous accounts of truth in those early years. Yet in the later work, his position emerges with more clarity and firmness: the earliest Greeks experienced Being as "primordial truth" as *aletheia* as emergence/self-showing/shining forth. In other words, for Heidegger, the principal "locus" of "truth" is Being itself, and not the human being. In the narrative he unfolded, it is Plato in particular who subtly shifted attention to the human knower in the matter of truth, and Aristotle followed in kind with the notion that truth is properly to be found in the "judgment." Even so, Heidegger appreciated the complexity of the work of both Greek thinkers, and he often found evidence of the earlier Greek experience of Being as "truth itself" in their thinking. Nevertheless, the subtle shift to the human "knower" in both Plato and Aristotle was discernible – and decisive in shaping all subsequent metaphysical thinking about "truth." In other words, the *aletheia*-character of Being was already to some degree "forgotten" prior to Descartes.

Yet, to be sure, this "forgottenness" became more acute in Descartes's thinking, which rendered things as static objects for a foundational human "subject," and it culminated in the thinking of the modern philosophy of consciousness in which things took on the character of mere mental objects or representations. The human "subject" or "mind" was thereby installed not only as the principal "locus" of truth, but also as the sole "source" of being and truth. It was in this Cartesian-Kantian-Husserlian philosophical climate of thinking that Heidegger sought to raise anew "the Being-question." Yet, as we observed earlier, it required of Heidegger many years of thinking – and *Holzwege* – to find a way out of the modern transcendental framework.

But he did. Heidegger ultimately found his way to his original and distinctive position: Being is "truth" in the first place as dynamic emergence and self-showing, that is, as *physis* and *aletheia*. This is the leading theme of his masterwork *Introduction to Metaphysics* (1935) and of his commentaries on Plato and Aristotle and on the sayings of the earliest Greek thinkers Parmenides, Heraclitus, and Anaximander from the late 1930s into the 1940s. In GA 97, we find numerous entries that state and restate this breakthrough position. For example, we read this "observation" (*Anmerkung*) from 1946–7:

> *Aletheia* is not a name for *veritas*, but rather for *esse*.
>
> (GA 97: 257)

This is one simple line that speaks to a whole history of philosophical thinking. I have examined the matter in some detail in *Heidegger's Way of Being*,[3] but, in brief, it was the medieval thinker Thomas Aquinas in particular who consolidated the position that, for Aristotle, "truth" (in Latin, *veritas*) properly resides only in the intellect, whether human or divine. Aquinas thereby rejected the position, suggested by Augustine and other earlier authors, that "truth" belongs in the first place to "being" (*esse*). For Heidegger, Aquinas's reading of Aristotle was clear evidence of the intensification of the "forgottenness" of the *aletheic* character of Being during the medieval period. His entry in the notebook thus states his novel position in a succinct and elegant manner: The ancient Greek *Ur*-word *aletheia* is not a name for "truth" understood in the traditional metaphysical manner as proper to the intellect (*veritas*), but rather it is, in the first place, the name for being (*esse*). Being is "primordial truth" as the emerging of what is emergent. Being is/as *Aletheia*.

In the same section of GA 97, he furthers this theme in another entry:

> To think Being aletheically means to experience that and how *Aletheia* is as the revealing of the beginning of the unfolding of *Seyn* [crossed out] = the unfolding of *physis*.   (261)

Again, the task is to think Being *aletheically*, and this is precisely what the earliest Greek thinkers gave us to think, but which was lost from view in the refocusing of our attention on the human knower with Plato and Aristotle. Furthermore, to think Being as *Aletheia* (and in this period Heidegger often capitalized the *Ur*-Greek words as names for Being) is to think "the unfolding of *physis*." In other words, Being as *aletheia* as "primordial truth" refers first and foremost to the temporal arising and emergence and showing forth of all things – and this is also *physis*, as he had so clearly shown in *Introduction to Metaphysics* (1935) and in the 1943 lecture course on Heraclitus. I have brought his position in these texts into high relief in Chapters 4 and 5 of *Heidegger's Way of Being*, but there is also helpful supplementary material to be found in Heidegger's gloss on his *Introduction to Metaphysics* in GA 73.1, which was more recently published. There, for instance, in the section titled "The Being-question and the Disempowering of *physis*," he observes that "to *physis* belongs unconcealedness," and he emphasizes that "Being unfolds as true-(being). Being is *the* truth as such." He continues that what we no longer see as clearly as the earliest Greeks is this:

> the fullness and simplicity of this *truthing of physis itself* [*aletheuein der physis selbst*].   (GA: 73.1: 133)

The "disempowering" of *aletheia* as *physis* (and *physis* as *aletheia*) largely begins, he states, with the shift in thinking in Aristotle to the "*psyche*" of the human being as the proper site of "truth" and thus "the later object-subject relation is here [with Aristotle] already prepared" (133).

These entries in GA 97, then, only restate and amplify the central position that he had worked out and laid out for at least a decade prior. In another entry, he sets the record straight once more about the proper aim of *Being and Time*:

> The meditation on the essence of truth in *Being and Time* and in the subsequent writings and lecture courses since then is by no means prompted by the question concerning the truth of cognition, and also not by a discussion of the truth of beings, but rather singularly by a thinking of the truth of Being.　　　　　(GA 97: 264)

And to this he adds the crucial point: to think "the truth of Being" is to think that "*physis* is Being in the sense of emergence. But emergence is in essence revealing, [that is], *Aletheia*" (264).

There are a number of other entries in the volume that speak to this same fundamental theme of his later work, and there is no need to examine all of them in detail.[4] Yet one especially instructive entry from 1948 tells us how far Heidegger believed he had come from Husserl's transcendental approach to the matter of Being. The great shortcoming of Husserl's transcendental idealism was that it could never fulfill the promise of getting to "the things themselves"; his was a philosophical method that entirely missed "the experience of *Aletheia*." In fact, Heidegger writes that Husserl "closed himself" to just such an experience:

> "That something shows itself forth from it itself" – is not only another formulation of the principle of proper description. In that phrase there speaks already the turning of thinking into *Aletheia* as the essential feature of Being itself in the sense of presencing. About all of this Husserl not only knows nothing, in fact he closes himself to it (*er sperrt sich dagegen*).　　　　　(GA 97: 442)

One might consider this a harsh observation, but we need to keep in mind that Heidegger is, in effect, also being harsh with himself, that is, with his own failure in *Being and Time*. Husserl, his teacher, had perhaps glimpsed the core matter, but he persisted in the modern manner of measuring out Being from the human being; that is, his focus remained on subjectivity in the "constitution" of the phenomenon. As we have observed, the early Heidegger was tempted along this way, too, but certainly after *Being and Time* – and as reflected in these notebooks – he clearly came to understand *Aletheia* as another name for Being itself. The *phainomenon* is not merely a "constituted" content for ever more rigorous consideration and description, but rather a vibrant temporal emergence: Being as *aletheia* – as *physis*. Husserl, according to Heidegger, missed this altogether and, in fact, for whatever reasons, actively "closed himself" against precisely *this exposure to the experience of Being as aletheia* – an experience which, as Heidegger also suggests here, would have turned Husserl out of the certainty and security of his transcendental-phenomenological program.

On the matter of Being as *physis* as *aletheia*, the many "observations" in GA 97 do not break new ground, as we have noted, but they do give us further evidence of the central importance of this motif in his thinking in the 1940s. He had found in the *Ur*-words of the earliest Greek thinkers a way out of the transcendental approach to Being that had ensnared him in *Being and Time*. His entries in this volume time and again seek to counter the transcendental-phenomenological inflection that it is the human being who is the "source" of Being and truth. Rather, as with the ancient Greeks, it must be recognized that Being, not the human being, is the "source" of unconcealment and concealment, no matter what our own activity of unconcealing and concealing. Thus:

> Unconcealment unfolding as Being; Being is the whence – whereunto and wherein of the unfolding of revealing-concealing.
>
> (GA 97: 456)

III.   Being as *Aletheia* as Independent of the Relation with Human Beings

One additional entry in GA 97 regarding this core theme of Being as *Aletheia* stands out because it brings into even sharper relief the radicality of Heidegger's position in relation to any transcendental or quasi-transcendental perspective. What we have been taking note of is the originality and distinctiveness of the later Heidegger's understanding of Being as "primordial truth" as temporal self-showing and shining forth. We could point to places in the early work where Heidegger approached this later understanding of Being, but, again, his early work was limited and inhibited by the transcendental framework he had adopted from Husserl. His early statements – such as in *Being and Time*, where he states that Being is only insofar as there is Dasein or that there is "truth" only insofar as there is Dasein – clearly reflected the extent to which his early thinking was captured by the transcendental positioning. Heidegger recognized this, and his dissatisfaction with his approach in *Being and Time* is in evidence in the notebooks (GA 94). Admittedly, however, Heidegger in the notebooks is not always forthright about his discontent with his own approach and is rather inclined to blame readers and critics for mistaking *Being and Time* as an "idealism" of some kind. Nevertheless, we cannot but hear in many of his entries in GA 94 his personal frustration with the framing of the *Seinsfrage* in *Being and Time* and his urgent call for a dramatic "leap" in thinking.

This "leap" took several forms in the later work. Some commentators have shown how it gave rise to his "Beyng-historical thinking" of the 1930s and especially in *Beiträge*. Yet my principal concern has been to show how Heidegger leapt ahead to the theme of Being as *physis* and *aletheia* beginning in the early 1930s – and continuing to the end of his life. He left behind the transcendental elements of *Being and Time* by realizing the full implications of his earliest intuition about ancient Greek thinking, namely, that the temporal *emergence* of all things ontologically precedes and exceeds the "constituting" activity of transcendental subjectivity. Henceforth, after the "turn" we may say, he never ceased emphasizing the priority and primacy of Being in relation to the human being.

This is not to say that Heidegger left behind his concern with the correlation of Being and the human being. This concern remained a constant, but what did change was his characterization of the correlation. In the later work, he abjured the transcendental understanding of the correlation, which is still in evidence in *Being and Time*, that Being is dependent upon the human being. His awakening (or reawakening) to the priority and primacy of Being in relation to the human being put this transcendental dependence into radical question, and the later Heidegger found different ways to affirm the "independence" (*Unabhängigkeit*) of Being as *physis* as *aletheia* in relation to the human being, even as he continued to speak about Being's "need" of the human being.[5] In the later work especially, "need" is not "dependence." The unending temporal self-showing and shining forth of Being as *physis* as *aletheia* is not in need of the human being in the strict sense, yet we may say that the human being is "needed" only as a mirror reflecting back in language the inexhaustible resplendence of Being's manifestation. He had put this very clearly in 1941:

> In the scope of the time when Being appropriates primordiality in the open and gives to be known and preserved the nobility of its freedom to itself, and consequently, its independence [*Unabhän-gigkeit*] as well, Being needs the reflected radiance of a shining forth of its essence in the truth.   (GA 6.2: 441)

It is in this same text that he refers to Being's "pure neeed-lessness" (*reine Unbedürftigkeit*). The radicality of Heidegger's later position on Being as *physis* as *aletheia* lies, then, in this: Being is not strictly speaking dependent upon the human being as the site or dative, the "to-whom," of Being's unending temporal emergence and unconcealedness. Not surprisingly, therefore, in the notebooks in an entry dated from 1948, we find him venturing just this point in a particularly bold and striking manner:

> *Aletheia* – unconcealedness; it is [*aletheia* – unconcealedness] is shown to be the unfolding region of everything that comes-to-presence, then one immediately seeks a substrate for it and asks: unconcealed "for" whom? – as if the free of the clearing [*Lichtung*] already had to be accommodated as well.   (GA 97: 458)

Of course, this is *precisely* the kind of statement of the later Heidegger that is so disconcerting to those who are committed to a "transcendental-phenomenological Heidegger." And yet – we must take these statements (and no doubt many additional ones in the later notebooks that have not yet been published) into account if we are to understand the trajectory of his thinking after the 1920s. The notebooks help us understand in yet another way the considerable distance that separates the later Heidegger from the Heidegger of *Being and Time*. There is a "unity" to Heidegger's thought, of course; but it cannot be properly discerned or appreciated if we do not recognize the significant changes and developments in his thinking over time.

Concluding Thought

It would not be surprising that even in a few short years the *Black Notebooks* will be largely set aside in favor of returning to Heidegger's major writings and lecture courses. Even so, as I have tried to show in this focused chapter, these notebooks, including the ones that have not yet been published, will be of some value in shedding more light on his central philosophical themes and on the development of his thinking. Admittedly, as has been already (too) much discussed, several of the entries in the volumes that have been published thus far do not reflect well on Heidegger the person, but then again – and let us not overlook this – there are also ample entries that remind us of the brilliance of Heidegger the thinker and the lyricism of Heidegger the poet of the manifestation of Being:

No matter how the unleashed distortion of everything runs riot, there remains to the knowing the mature calm of the mountain, the gathered illumination of the meadows, the silent flight of the falcon, the bright cloud in the expansive sky – that wherein the majestic stillness of the farthest nearness of Beyng has already announced itself.   (GA 94:304)

3 Heidegger's Manifold Thinking of Being

In Honor of Professor William J. Richardson, S.J.

This chapter is in tribute to my teacher and mentor and one of the earliest and most preeminent of Heidegger scholars, William J. Richardson, who passed away at the age of 96 in 2016. As a teacher, Prof. Richardson was intense and inspiring; as a mentor, he uplifted his students by challenging them, always seeking to draw out the best they could offer; as a man, he was a rock of integrity. As we both grew older, I was also fortunate to become his colleague and friend, and we presented together on Heidegger's thought on several different occasions. I was honored that Prof. Richardson contributed the Foreword to my first book *Engaging Heidegger*. Bill (as I knew him) was always both proud and humbled that Heidegger had written the Preface to his book – and I will always feel the same way about Bill's Foreword to my book.

Prof. Richardson's great work of scholarship, *Heidegger: Through Phenomenology to Thought*, was first published in 1963 (Netherlands: Martinus Nijhoff). He had many wonderful stories about the research and writing of the book and about his decisive meeting with Heidegger in 1959. He told these stories with great drama and relish, and I shared many a glass of sherry and wine with him in conversation. Bill was very much like Socrates in the Platonic Dialogues: He would listen intently but then always lean in with yet another question. And how his eyes sparkled when he did so!

Bill always gratefully recalled Heidegger's personal generosity and graciousness toward him, and he also remained struck to the very end of his life by how profoundly calm and meditative Heidegger became when he peered out into the wooded landscape from the window of his study. In those moments, Bill said to me many times, Heidegger took on "the countenance of a nature mystic." Prof. Richardson's groundbreaking research brought into view the centrality of the *Seinsfrage* in Heidegger's lifetime of thinking, and his book stands as a remarkable scholarly achievement. At present, however, I simply wish to call attention to Prof. Richardson's opening words to the main part of his book, because these poetic lines tell us as much about his own *Denkweg* as about Heidegger's:

> There is a long and winding way that leads from Reichenau to Todtnauberg. It is Martin Heidegger's way. Past the moor and through the fields, it wends its way over the hills, only to wander now this way, now that, along uncharted forest trails. Yet for all its meandering, it moves in a single direction; it is but a single way. The purpose of these pages is to trace in some measure that way in order to raise the question whether others may walk it too.

Heidegger concluded the famous Preface to Richardson's masterful work of scholarship by stating three times that "a manifold thinking" (*ein mehrfältiges Denken*) is called for in calling forth the core matter for thought, and he expressed a "wish" for the book – a wish that has been fulfilled many times over since its publication in 1963 – that it set into motion this "manifold thinking" of the core matter, which "by reason of its very simplicity, abounds in hidden plenitude." In what follows, I offer a detailed overview of Heidegger's *manifold thinking of Being* in honor of Prof. Richardson's memory and his enduring legacy to Heidegger studies.

I. Heidegger's Core Concern: The Primacy of Being

In Heidegger's own view, stated innumerable times over the course of his long lifetime of thinking, the matter of Being was the fundamental matter of his thought (*die Sache selbst*). Whether in the early, middle, or late years, he maintained that the question of Being (*die Seinsfrage*) was the question that first and foremost propelled his thinking and sustained his thinking. In a letter dated 20 October 1966 to Manfred Frings, who was the convener of a "Heidegger Symposium" in Chicago, Heidegger wrote:

> I would be most delighted if it were possible to orient the discussion at once – in the first moments of the symposium – purely and decisively toward the matter (*die Sache*). In this way, there could develop, instead of a "Heidegger Symposium," a *Colloquium on the Question of Being*. For it is this question – and it alone – that determines the path of my thinking and its boundaries.
>
> (GA 16: 684)[1]

Nevertheless, he did not always approach the matter of Being in a direct manner; rather, he brought to language a rich array of names and phrases, each of which attempted to bring into view a fundamental feature of the "*Ur*-phenomenon" that the earliest Greek thinkers had named "Being."

What we may glean from his life-long reflections and meditations is that Being (*Sein*) lets beings (*das Seiende*) be in their beingness (*die Seiendheit*). As he put this simply and elegantly in 1945: "Now Beyng is that which lets each and every being be what it is and how it is, precisely because Beyng is the freeing that lets every single thing rest in its abiding fullness; that is, Beyng safeguards each and every thing" (GA 73.1: 879). In other words, Being, which is not a being itself, is the temporal-spatial way whereby and wherein all beings issue forth, come to be, in their beingness, that is, in their full appearance or "full look" (the ancient Greek philosophical terms *eidos* or *morphe*). Being is the pure emerging of all that emerges (*physis*). Being is the pure manifesting of all that is manifest (*aletheia*). Being is the pure laying-out and gathering of all that is (the primordial *Logos*). This understanding of Being, although already in evidence in the early work, came into fullest view in his writings and reflections after *Being and Time*.

II. A Note on the Orthographical Issue in the English Scholarship

The Heidegger scholarship in English has for decades used the capitalized word "Being" to refer to his original and distinctive understanding of the age-old term. As Prof. Richardson pointed out, this capitalization is meant to indicate that Heidegger's fundamental concern is not to be confused with the traditional metaphysical concern with "being" as "beingness," that is, with what Plato and Aristotle and the subsequent metaphysical tradition of thinking referred to as the timeless "form" or "essence" of a particular thing, the "being(ness)" of a being. Since all nouns in the German language are capitalized, Heidegger did not have at his disposal this graphical option for making this crucial distinction. Nevertheless, he found other ways to indicate the distinction, employing, for example, the archaic German word "*Seyn*" or sometimes even writing the word "*Sein*" and crossing it out. In addition, he often did make use of capital letters in writing the Greek words *Physis*, *Aletheia*, and *Logos* (as names for *Sein*), which gives us an important clue.

This is not to say, however, that he was always very careful with his use of the word *Sein*; sometimes it marked his fundamental concern, and sometimes it was only the indicator of the "beingness" of metaphysical thinking. Admittedly, one of the difficulties of reading Heidegger is that from text to text – and sometimes even from passage to passage – it is not clear whether he is referring to the *Sein* that is his ownmost concern or to the *Sein* spoken of in the metaphysical tradition. Even so, he was much more careful and precise with certain specific phrases. In his universe of terms, *Sein selbst* (Being itself), *Sein als solches* (Being as such), and *Sein als Sein* (Being as Being) are always used to mark or indicate the *Grund*-question and the fundamental matter for thought. In the German, as well as in English, these expressions may still invite confusion, however, since, for example, the expression "*Sein als Sein*" also translates Aristotle's inquiry into *on hei on*, "being as being," which became the core topic of metaphysics and was certainly not Heidegger's primary concern.

The English-language convention of using the capital B in all these phrases avoids this possible confusion, but at a cost perhaps. Some commentators have complained that the capitalization disguises the temporal character of Being. Yet this is certainly not intended by the written convention. More recently, some commentators have employed the alternative convention of rendering Heidegger's *Sein* (*Seyn*) with the hyphenated word "be-ing." This word form has its advantages, but it introduces the oddity and awkwardness of writing Heidegger's key terms as "be-ing itself," "be-ing as such," and "be-ing as be-ing." Overall, with the proper qualifications in place, it remains a reasonable option to continue to use the long-standing English-language convention of writing "Being" to mark Heidegger's *Sein*, and it is the convention followed in this book. The chief difficulty with not employing any graphical convention whatsoever is that his original and distinctive understanding of *Sein*, rendered simply as "being," may remain indistinguishable from, and likely confused with, "being" as it was understood for so many centuries in the Western philosophical tradition.

III.   The Ambiguity of the Word "Being"

On several occasions in his later work (for example, GA 8, GA 40, GA 78), Heidegger brought to light and reflected upon the ambiguity or "twofoldness" of the Greek participle *on*, or in the older form, *eon*. On the one hand, *on*, "this participle of participles" as he referred to it, may convey the nominal meaning of "a being"; on the other hand, it may be heard in its verbal sense of "to be," the Greek infinitive form *einai*. In all his discussions of the grammar and etymology of the Greek word *on*, as well as of the German word *Sein*, he emphasized that the crucial matter is that the inherent ambiguity of this *Ur*-word reveals the fundamental matter for thought itself (*die Sache selbst*), namely, "the ontological difference" between Being (that which lets all beings be) and beings (in their beingness) (GA 40: 56–79; GA 78: 37–51; 211–14). The classical metaphysical tradition of thinking focused its attention on "beings" (*on* in the form of *onta*, beings in their beingness) and lost sight of "Being" (*einai*); thereby the primordial "difference" between Being and beings was "forgotten."

IV. Being as *Physis*

A key to understanding Heidegger's transition to his mature understanding of *Sein* after *Being and Time* is his turn in the late 1920s and early 1930s to the ancient Greek notion of *physis*. His reading of *physis* as emergence, arising, upsurgence, irruption, manifestation appears to have been crucial in his leaving behind once and for all the Husserlian transcendental-phenomenological manner of framing and characterizing *Sein* and embarking upon his own distinctive ways of approaching the matter of Being.

For Heidegger – a point that he would make repeatedly over the next four and half decades of his life – what Husserl and the other modern transcendental thinkers had missed was the extraordinary power and vibrancy of the *emerging* of all beings and things. The subjectivism or, perhaps more precisely, the *subjectism* of their basic philosophical position had rendered Being mute, and Heidegger was determined to allow Being "to speak" again. This meant that it was necessary to overcome the transcendental-phenomenological bias that it is the human *logos* that measures out Being and to recognize and appreciate once again that Being measures out the human being in the first place (for example, GA 10: 166; GA 55: 168–71). In the compelling philosophical narrative that Heidegger began to tell especially in the early 1930s, it was the ancient Greeks and their thinkers – including to some extent Plato and Aristotle – who experienced Being as *physis* as opening and showing and emerging, in effect, "the truthing of *physis* itself" (*aletheuein der physis selbst*, GA 73.1: 133). The Greeks, he often remarked, dwelled in the midst of manifestness and were open and transparent to the "address" of Being, that is, to the "appeal" of Being to the human being to correspond (*Entsprechung*) in art and word.

Heidegger's great insight into – or at least his signature reading of – the ancient Greek notion of *physis* informed his understanding of Being from the 1930s until his death in 1976. In the 1930s, a major statement is his 1935 *Introduction to Metaphysics* (IM), arguably his masterwork of the 1930s and philosophically more significant and enduring than his private meditations composed as *Beiträge zur Philosophie: (Vom Ereignis)* (1936–8). In IM, he richly, poetically, evokes the pure "emerging itself" that is *physis*, and he concludes in no uncertain terms: "*Physis* is Being itself, by virtue of which beings first become and remain observable" (GA 40:17).

Everything, including humans and the gods, emerges from out of *physis*/Being, and this primordial unfolding "includes both 'becoming' as well as 'being[ness]' in the narrower sense of fixed continuity." In other words, *physis* unfolds beings in such a way that both the movement (becoming) of beings and the abiding and perduring (beingness) of beings may now be seen as but two aspects of the single temporal-spatial way or process. Thus for Heidegger, the age-old metaphysical distinction between "becoming" (potency) and "being" (act, actuality) is "grounded" or "unified" in the onefold that is Being itself as *physis*. This point is subsequently fully unfolded in his statement *On the Essence and Concept of Physis in Aristotle's Physics B, I*, composed in 1939.

Being as *physis* is temporal manifestation, but manifestation bears within it – shows up for us – the dimension of withholding or "concealment." According to Heidegger, this is the abiding lesson to be learned from fragment 123 of Heraclitus, *physis kryptesthai philei*, which is usually translated into English as "nature loves to hide." Over the course of many years and many texts, he employed a variety of translations to make the point again and again that manifestation intrinsically includes this dimension of reserve that must be acknowledged and honored by us: "the *kryptesthai* of *physis* is not to be overcome, not to be stripped from *physis*" (GA 9: 301). There is a depth to manifestation – to Being as *physis* – that is never exhausted by our saying, language, meaning, no matter how broadly these may be construed. In 1949, he made this point simply: "This truth of Being is not exhausted in Dasein" (GA 9: 373–4).

V. Being as *Aletheia*

Also crucial in his transition to his later thinking about Being was his ongoing reflections during the 1920s on the ancient Greek notion of *aletheia* and his progressive realization that, for the Greeks, *aletheia* was, in the first place, a characterization of Being and not of the human *logos*. He found confirmation for this position in his reading of Aristotle's *Metaphysics Theta*, 10 at 1051b. "With this chapter," he remarked, "Aristotle's treatise reaches its proper end; indeed, the whole of Aristotle's philosophy attains its 'highest point'" (GA 33: 11–12). For Heidegger, *aletheia* ("truth" understood in an originary and primordial manner) names, first and foremost, the peculiar and proper manifestness of Being and not the manifestive activity of the human being, which had been maintained in one way or another in the long tradition of philosophical thinking in the West.

Prof. Richardson had detected Heidegger's breakthrough to this position in the 1930 lecture "On the Essence of Truth." From the 1930s onward, Heidegger maintained that "*aletheia* ... is the fundamental feature of Being itself" (GA 55: 175). This position – that Being is *aletheia* in the first place – is a hallmark of the originality and distinctiveness of his thinking, and especially of his thinking after *Being and Time*. Heidegger observed that thinking about *aletheia* in this way is too difficult and too "strange" for contemporary philosophy, which by virtue of the most deeply ingrained and stubborn habit of thinking, insists on maintaining that the proper locus of "the truth of Being" is the human *logos*. The continuing challenge for thinking is to take up and take to heart that "truth abides in everything that abides" (GA 54: 242), that "Being is *the* truth as such" (GA 73.1: 133, his italics), and that "truth as self-revealing belongs to Being itself" (GA 9: 301). The recurring theme of Heidegger's later work is that Being "is" *physis* "is" *aletheia*, or put paratactically, as he was fond of doing, Being: *physis*: *aletheia*: the Same (*das Selbe*).

VI. Being as the Primordial *Logos*

It is arguable that the core of the later Heidegger's thinking concerning Being may be found in his lecture courses on the earliest Greek thinkers – Parmenides, Heraclitus, and Anaximander – in the early 1940s. In these lecture courses, he worked out in especially creative ways the themes of Being as *physis* (Heraclitus, 1943) and Being as *aletheia* (Parmenides, 1942–3). The motif of Being as the primordial *Logos* (*der ursprüngliche Logos*) was brought to fullest expression in his 1944 lecture course on Heraclitus. He is ardent in maintaining that originally the ancient Greek word *logos* did not principally "belong" to the human being or to any activity or capability of the human being, but rather to Being itself:

> The *logos* of the customarily so-called logic is, as statement and saying, an activity and capability of the human being. This *logos* belongs to the being that the human being is. The *Logos* [Heidegger uses the capital *lambda*, in the same way that he also often wrote *Aletheia* and *Physis*] of which Heraclitus speaks is the gathered and the gathering as the One that unifies everything, and not as any feature within a being. This *Logos* is the primordial gathering that preserves the being as the being that it is. *This Logos is Being itself wherein all beings unfold.*   (GA 55: 278, my italics)

Furthermore, he boldly maintains that the primordial *Logos* is "indeed a kind of saying and word" (259) and also "a kind of speech and voice" (244), yet, lest there be any confusion, he insists that this *Logos* "is manifestly not the voice of a human being" (244). Being as the *Logos* is the "saying" – "word," "speech," "voice" – as the laying out, opening up, clearing, showing, shining forth of all that is. Our task as human beings is to "hearken" to this primordial "voice" of manifestation and bring forth what is "said" into our own "saying." We correspond to the primordial "saying," and our correspondence (*Entsprechung*) is what Heraclitus named *homologein*. His elucidations are dense and difficult, admittedly, but they are not mystifying. They represent Heidegger's original and compelling way of recovering the experience of the manifestness of Being that, in his view, had been lost or "forgotten" in the thoroughgoing subjectism of the modern philosophy of consciousness, including Husserl's transcendental-phenomenology. His meditations on the primordial *Logos*, along with his readings of *physis* and *aletheia* and several other Greek *Ur*-words, such as *hen, kosmos, zoe*, all sought to awaken us to the *experience* of "the truth of Being" (*die Wahrheit des Seins*).

VII. Being as the "Ground" of History

In *Beiträge* and the *Beiträge*-related manuscripts, Heidegger pursues a "Beyng-historical thinking," which attempts to think Being (as *Seyn*, Beyng) as it unfolds or issues forth in the various historical "epochs" of the thinking of "beingness." The "first inception" among the ancient Greeks glimpsed Being as pure giving and granting, and the "other inception," which is breaking in upon human beings in the present time, retrieves the first inception and brings into fresh language the giving, letting, appropriating character of Beyng itself, namely, as *Ereignis.*

What is important to emphasize here is that although Beyng/ Being issues forth in the different historical epochs of the thinking of beingness (*Seiendheit*), Beyng/Being itself is not reducible to this history of epochs. That is, Beyng/Being is the pure primordial temporal emerging that gives rise to the history of epochs, or to put this another way, Beyng/Being is the groundless "ground" of epochal history. In 1941, he states: "The history of Being is neither the history of the human being and of humanity, nor the history of the human relation to beings and to Being. The history of Being is Being itself, and only Being" (GA 6.2: 447).

In his later 1955–6 lecture course "The Principle of Ground," he reprises this theme in terms of the "dispensation" (*Geschick*) of Being and maintains that Being may be understood as the "ground" as the temporal laying-out and gathering way (Heraclitus's *physis, aletheia, Logos*), but not as any metaphysical first cause, first principle, or sufficient reason. Being is the pure arising that is without "why" and is like a child at "play," as he reads fragment 52 of Heraclitus. Being as (groundless) ground gives rise to world-historical epochs, but is not exhausted by them: "Being and ground is not an empty oneness; rather, it is the *concealed fullness* of what first comes to light in the dispensation of Being as the history of Western thinking" (GA 10: 165).

In "The Saying of Anaximander," he emphasizes the irreducibility of Being-as-giving to its historical dispensations, and in so doing, he also sharply diverges from Husserl on the meaning and significance of the term *epoché*:

> We may call this clearing holding-itself-back of the truth of Being's essencing the *epoché* of Being. Yet this word borrowed from the language of the Stoics does not mean, as with Husserl, the methodical bracketing of the thetic act of consciousness in objectifying. The *epoché* of Being belongs to Being itself ... From out of the *epoché* of Being comes the epochal essencing of its dispensation, in which proper world history consists.   (GA 5: 333)

VIII.   Being as Time

From the outset of his path of thinking, Heidegger was concerned to show the temporal character of Being, yet he often admitted that his early efforts, and especially in *Being and Time*, were inadequate. In the Preface to Prof. Richardson's book, he observed: "The ekstatic-horizonal temporality [of Dasein] delineated in *Being and Time* is not by any means already the most proper attribute of time that must be sought in answer to the question of Being" (GA 11: 147). The later Heidegger had a clearer view that the time-character of Being is not reducible to the temporality projected by the human being. Being-as-time or Being-Time is not reducible to "being" as it is constituted by inner time-consciousness – and this shows once again the measure of his distance from Husserl's transcendental-phenomenological perspective. Heidegger's later approach was to emphasize how Being unfolds the human being and thereby *temporalizes* the human being. Our temporality is what it is only because we are the "there" of Being itself that "times."

This later approach is in evidence, for example, in a commentary on Anaximander's fragment in the 1941 lecture course "Basic Concepts" (GA 51). Anaximander's *Ur*-word *apeiron* tells us, according to Heidegger's bold reading (107–23), how "Being lets beings be." As beings issue forth, they are inclined to perdure in their presence, even to the extent of fixity and permanence; yet there is also at work an overarching countervailing movement to repel this fixity or "limit" (*peras, Grenze*) and move all beings out of their presence. Being as the *apeiron* – that is, *a-peiron* (the repelling of *peras*, limit) – is the movement or "passage" that requires of all beings both arrival into – and departure from – their proper presence. In this way, then, "passage" characterizes Being itself, or as he also states it, "*Being itself is lingering, presencing*" (121, his italics). And this thus clarifies the relation of Being to time as expressed in Anaximander's fragment: Being is the temporal allotment of beings. We do not, he claims, attain to an understanding of the genuine character of time by saying "time is." Rather, we get closer when we say, "It is time." Thus, to crystallize Heidegger's view, we may put it this way: *It is time* for the flowers to bloom, the rain to fall, the air to chill. *It is time* that all things, including ourselves, come – and go. We do not allot time; Being-as-time allots to us our time upon the earth and under the sky in the company of all other beings.

IX. Being as *Ereignis* and *Lichtung*

Heidegger's terms of art, *Ereignis* and *Lichtung*, require more extensive treatment than is possible in this overview, and for fuller discussions, see my *Engaging Heidegger* and *Heidegger's Way of Being*. Still, it is necessary to address the matter of the relation of these terms to Being. In *Beiträge* and the *Beiträge*-related manuscripts, he often states that "*Ereignis* is Beyng" or that "Beyng is *Ereignis*," and he also frequently cites "Beyng as *Ereignis*" or "*Ereignis* as Beyng." These private manuscripts do not at all suggest that he subordinated Being/Beyng to *Ereignis*. This is also the case in his later *Ereignis*-writings of the late 1950s and early 1960s. Most notably, in his 1962 lecture "Time and Being," he brings his remarks on *Ereignis* to a conclusion by stating that "the sole aim of this lecture is to bring into view Being itself as *Ereignis*" (GA 14: 26).

Equally explicit are his remarks about *die Lichtung*, "the clearing." In *Letter on Humanism* (1947), he offers a clarification of his earlier position in *Being and Time* and firmly maintains: "But the clearing itself is Being" (GA 9: 332). This statement informs all of his reflections on "the clearing" in the later work. The human being "belongs" to the clearing, is "the guardian of the clearing," *but is not the whole of the clearing, not the clearing itself* (GA 89: 663; ZS: 223). In addition, at several points in his later writings, he yokes his other distinctive names for the *Ur*-phenomenon to Being itself. Thus, with respect to *Es gibt*, he comments in the *Letter on Humanism* that "the 'it' [*es*] that here 'gives' [*gibt*] is Being itself" (GA 9: 334). In the Parmenides lecture course, he italicizes the statement, *"the open is Being itself"* (GA 54: 224). And in the 1944 lecture course on Heraclitus, he reads both the region (*Gegend*) and the expanse (*Weite*) as naming Being itself (GA 55: 337).

X.   The Relation of Being to the Human Being: The Independence of Being

In the later work, Heidegger more often referred to "the human being" (*der Mensch*) rather than to "Dasein," his word of choice for the unfolding (or "essencing") of the human being that he employed in *Being and Time* and in the early work generally. One reason for this change appears to be that he had come to understand *Da-sein* in a broader and richer way to refer to the essencing of every being, and not just the human being, from out of Being. Consequently, the term "human Dasein" would be more in keeping with the basic themes of the later Heidegger. Nevertheless, in the later work, he did occasionally refer to "Dasein" as the name for the human being, and especially when he was recalling key passages from his early work.

In one sense, the matter here is simple: Heidegger was centrally concerned with the "relation" (*Bezug, Beziehung*) between Being and the human being. This relation is special and even exalted for Heidegger because it is the human being who clears the clearing in a privileged manner; that is, the human being is able to correspond to Being in "language," in art and word. Generally, his reflections circle around this core concern: not Being alone, not the human being alone, but the relation between Being and the human being. Parmenides' dictum that Being (*einai*) and thinking (*noein*) belong together guided Heidegger's thinking from beginning to end.

This much may be clear, yet some of Heidegger's formulations have given rise to confusion. For example, he was fond of stating that Being "needs" (*braucht*) the human being. But what exactly does this mean? He did not intend this as a metaphysical statement to the effect that there is Being (emergence, manifestation of all beings and things) *only if* there is the human being. He was not at all interested in advancing this kind of metaphysical idealism that would hold that the manifestation of everything depends upon the human being. In fact, he was often perfectly clear that Being does *not* depend upon the human being, that is, that Being is independent of the human being:

> Yet Being is never dependent upon existing humanity.
> (GA 6.2: 441)

> [Being as] "truth" is "independent" of the human being, since truth means the unfolding of what is true in the sense of unconcealedness.   (GA 88: 205)

> Being and the truth of Being is essentially beyond all human beings and every historical humanity.   (GA 54: 249)

> The human being for itself has no power over truth, which remains independent of the human being.   (GA 77: 147)

Some might, then, characterize Heidegger's formulation that Being "needs" the human being as "phenomenological." Yet "phenomenological" here could not refer to Husserl's particular and strict manner of approaching the matter, but rather, very broadly, to the fact that our access to Being is only through our Dasein. In other words, we might say that Heidegger wished to focus on the simple givenness that Being and the human being happen together: When we speak about Being, we are speaking, and when we speak, we are speaking about Being. Considered in this broadly "phenomenological" manner, then, the statement

"Being needs the human being" is simply his distinctive way of keeping the "relation" of Being and the human being foremost in view. Nevertheless, it does not follow from this that Being is thereby dependent upon the human being and reducible to "meaning" in a strictly transcendental-phenomenological manner. "Need" is not necessarily dependence. In fact, in 1941, Heidegger insisted on Being's "pure neeedlessness" (*reine Unbedürftigkeit*) and clarified Being's "independence" from the human being:

> In the scope of the time when Being appropriates primordiality in the open and gives to be known and preserved the nobility of its freedom to itself, and consequently, its independence [*Unabhängigkeit*] as well, Being needs the reflected radiance of a shining forth of its essence in the truth.   (GA 6.2: 441)

In other words, the unending temporal self-showing and shining forth of Being as *physis* as *aletheia* is not in need of the human being *in the strict sense*, yet we may say that the human being is "needed" only as a mirror reflecting back in language and art the inexhaustible resplendence of Being's emergence and manifestation.

To illustrate this point let us imagine Cezanne standing before Mont Sainte-Victoire and remarking to himself, "The truth of this mountain needs to be painted." The word "needs" in this sentence gets us close to the heart of what the later Heidegger was seeking to convey. The overwhelming showing, manifestation, shining forth of the mountain compels the human being to paint or poetize its "truth." In other words, the mountain "needs" the human being to show itself *as* a painting or a poem or as any work of art, all of which belong properly to the domain of the human being. Yet, surely, the "truth" of the mountain is not exhausted in the painting or the poem. Being as emergence is by no means exhausted by human correspondence. Cezanne painted Mont Sainte-Victoire over sixty times by some accounts – the mountain "needed" him to – but not once, let us again imagine, did he think to himself that he had exhausted – or that he ever could exhaust – the manifestation of the mountain. Again, in Heidegger's own words, "This truth of Being is not exhausted in Dasein" (GA 9: 373–4). To put this in more plain philosophical language, then, the later Heidegger was a *metaphysical realist* of a kind in that he maintained that both beings and Being (out of which beings arise) are "independent" of the human being; yet he was also always concerned that we not lose sight of the distinctive correspondence (Heraclitus's *homologein*) of the human being.

Concluding Thought

For the later Heidegger, Being is the "ever-emerging" and "ever-living" *kosmos* spoken of by Heraclitus in fragment 30. As Heidegger reflected on this fragment many times over several decades, he took very much to heart Heraclitus's words that "no god and no human being has brought forth" Being as *kosmos*. He called upon us to be ever more open, ever more transparent, to the shining forth and resplendence of Being. His translation of fragment 30 gave testimony to his life-long deepening meditation on the primacy of Being in relation to our Dasein:

> This *kosmos* here, insofar as it is the same for everyone and everything, no one of the gods and also no human being has brought forth; it always already was, and it is, and will be: inexhaustibly living fire, flaming up in measures, and in measures going out.
>
> (GA 15: 280)

4 Athena, Art, and Overcoming the Egoity of Our Age

The human being for itself has no power over truth, which remains
independent of the human being.

Heidegger, "Three in Conversation
on a Country Path," 1944–5 (GA 77: 147)

Even if no human being were to see them, the stars would shine forth
nonetheless.

Heidegger, citing approvingly Aristotle,
Metaphysics VII, 1041a (GA 15: 334)

There are many reasons to study Heidegger's thinking, but an
especially important one is to help free us from the many and
varied "subjectivisms" of the contemporary age, including the
persistent Cartesianism and Kantianism of classical phenomenology as inaugurated by Husserl. Husserl's basic position was
strongly inflected toward the dependence of "being" on human
subjectivity: "It is a being (*ein Sein*) that consciousness in its own
experiences posits, ... but *over and beyond this*, is nothing at all"
(*Ideas I*, §49). The later Heidegger refused all such human-centric
perspectives, and I have attempted to show the manifold dimen-
sions of his critique in both *Engaging Heidegger* and *Heidegger's
Way of Being*. His heralded turn to *Sein/Seyn* (henceforth, Being),
as he worked this out over the course of his lifetime of thinking,
represented a decisive turn away from all prevailing modern
versions of the human being as the measure of all things.

Yet rather than restate the case already made, I would like to consider the matter afresh and highlight several of his signature themes along the way. In 1967, Heidegger delivered an address to the Academy of Arts and Sciences in Athens, Greece, under the title "The Provenance of Art and the Determination of Thinking." This lecture is not well-known, and it has only recently been published in Heidegger's *Complete Works* (*Gesamtausgabe*).[1] The address is one of several that he delivered in the 1960s that speak to similar themes, yet what is especially notable in this particular talk is his appeal to the figure of the Greek goddess Athena to highlight the core matter of "*Aletheia*" and how *Aletheia* is not only the "provenance" of "art," but also "older," "more primordial," and "more enduring" than the human being and all that is brought forth as "art" by the human being. In other words, *Aletheia* (as Being), although correlated with the human being in the expanse of the time of human beings, is nonetheless *independent* of the human being. Yet let us approach this conclusion slowly by way of a consideration of the lecture text.

I. Athena Speaks

Heidegger opens the address by stating in a characteristic manner that the matter of the inception of the "arts and sciences" among the Greeks is not fundamentally an "historical" matter that lies in the distant past, but rather a matter – and an experience – that remains "present" to us. The task before us, he states, is to "meditate on the provenance of art in Hellas" (136/119). Note that he uses the word "Hellas," and not "Greece" (*Griechenland*), as he begins his reflection. This is his reminder, familiar to us from many other places in his work, that, in his view, we must peel back the layers of Romanized and Latinized thinking that have accrued over the centuries in order for us to arrive again at the originary matter for thought; thus, our seeking must find its way back not to Roman *Graecia*, but to *Hellas*. In the following line, he sets out the aim of the meditation: "We shall try to get a glimpse into the region (*Bereich*) that already prevails prior to all art and that first bestows to art its ownmost character" (136/119). This "region" that "prevails" and is "prior" to all art – and therefore "prior" to the human being – is "*A-letheia*," as he will tell us in due course, but at the outset he has already clearly signaled the destination of his thinking.

To proceed, he calls upon "the goddess Athena" for "counsel and guidance." This is not simply a polite rhetorical gesture to his Athenian hosts. The later Heidegger was deeply moved by the "invocation" to the gods or muses that opened the great poems of the ancient Greek poets such as Homer and Pindar. These ancient invocations honored the gods for their "wisdom" and expressed an abiding human humility to listen and learn – which Heidegger laments has been increasingly lost in the present "egoist" age.

The matter of the significance of "the gods" in the later Heidegger's thinking is complex, but we should at least keep in view that he always insisted that "the gods" are never mere projections of the human being; that is, "the gods," no less than we "mortals," emerge from out of Being, the temporal-spatial emerging/ unfolding "way" (or ontological process) wherein and whereby all beings issue forth and come to be. Certainly, for Heidegger, the "gods" or "divinities" are not traditional onto-theological timeless entities, for they, too, are "temporal" as they emerge from out of the temporal way itself – Being – their "source." Some recent readings of Heidegger – which are no more than variations of Husserl's transcendental idealism – are entirely off the mark to suggest that for the later Heidegger the human being is the "source" of "Being," and, accordingly, these readings are also mistaken in trying to settle the matter of "the gods" in his thinking by claiming them for the human being, that is, by claiming that "the gods" are only insofar as the human being is. Heidegger – at every turn – upends this kind of position. In this talk, not only does he "invoke" the goddess Athena, but he adds that even as we look to her for counsel and illumination on the core matter for thinking, we must ever keep in mind that "we cannot penetrate into the plenitude of her divinity" (136/119). What is more, he states, "We are only attempting to explore what Athena says to us about the provenance of art." He recalls that our human task is to be attentive and *listen* to "what Athena says." In other words, it is not simply humans who "say" and "speak"; the goddess "says" and "speaks," too.

Admittedly, what and how "the gods" "are" as they emerge from out of the Being-way, and what and how "the gods" "say" and "speak," are considerations that remain for us to reflect upon further – and this only testifies to the continuing resonance of Heidegger's thinking. Even so, let us recognize that what he opens for our thinking in such passages is altogether closed off in every kind of reductive human-centric reading that insists on positing the human being as the singular "source" of all "saying." In other words, what is lost in these reductive human-centric readings is Heidegger's abiding call for us to be "open" to how all things "speak" to us. As he had put this in a seminar in Le Thor a couple of years later in 1969: "The Greeks are those human beings who lived immediately (*unmittelbar*) in the manifestness of phenomena – through the specifically ek-static capacity of letting the phenomena *speak to them*, [yet] modern man, Cartesian man, *se solum alloquendo*, speaks only to himself."[2] For us to be "open" in this Greek way is for us to be "open" to hearing how the sea, the trees, the animals – all that is, even "the gods" and "muses" – how *everything* "speaks" to us.[3] Yet it seems that we are no longer listening – or we are listening only for what we need and demand to hear.

Heidegger recalls that Homer names Athena *polumetis*, "the manifold counselor" (136/119), the one who helps in many and varied ways. It is Athena who "prevails" over everything that human beings bring forth, and it is she who "dispenses her special counsel to humans who produce tools, vases, and jewels." All who are skilled and masters at crafting we may call a *technites*, but he cautions that "we understand this word in too limited a sense when we translate it as 'artisan.'" The *technites* is one whose activity "is guided by a comprehension whose name is *techne*," yet this word does not simply mean "a doing and making"; rather, *techne* is fundamentally "a form of knowing." This "knowing" is a seeing in advance of what is to be brought forth, and what is to be brought forth is not simply a crafted chair or sculpture or building – but also "a work of science or of philosophy, of poetry or of public rhetoric." In this way, then, "art is *techne*, but not *technicity* (*Technik*)," and "the artist is *technites*, but not a technician or even an artisan" (137/120).

Thus "art," according to Heidegger, is a kind of *techne*, and *techne* is a "knowing" that is a looking ahead to the creation and completion of *any work*. This "knowing" as a "looking ahead" therefore requires "exceptional vision and brightness and clarity," and again he invokes the goddess Athena, who is not only the manifold counselor, *polumetis*, but also well-known as the bright and shining one, *glaucopis*. He considers the Greek word *"glaucos"* and observes that the adjective *glaucos* usually refers to "the radiant gleaming (*das strahlende Glänzen*) of the sea, the stars, the moon, but also the shimmer of the olive tree" (137/120). The published translation opts for "lustre" to translate his word *Glänzen*, and this is acceptable, of course, but I think the word "gleaming" gets us much closer to the "shining forth" that he always had in view. In Chapter 2 of *Heidegger's Way of Being*, I highlight and discuss how this word *glänzen* is widely used by Heidegger and one of his most favored words in speaking of the "shining forth" of beings and of the Being-way itself – and not surprisingly, he himself had pointed out that this very word was widely used and highly favored by Hölderlin in the first place.[4]

Athena's "eyes" are *"glaucos,"* that is, "gleaming and illuminating." It is for this reason, he adds, that the owl, whose eyes are "fiery-blazing," has the name *he glaux* in Greek and is forever associated with her, "a sign of her essence." The owl's bright eyes are able to see at night as well, and, correspondingly, Athena's bright and gleaming glance is able to "make visible what is otherwise invisible" (120/137). Yet where is Athena's illuminating glance directed? What is the "invisible" she has in view? The clue, he says, is to be found on the sacred relief on the Acropolis museum where Athena appears as the *skeptomene*, "the meditating one."

What follows is a familiar motif but now unfolded in terms of Athena as the meditating one. Athena's glance is turned toward "the boundary stone, to the boundary." Athena's bright eyes watch over meditatively the "boundary" or "limit" of things, but this limit is not a mere limitation or marker for the end of something. Rather, "limit," understood in a genuinely Greek manner, is what determines something coming to be in its ownmost character and fullness. Indeed, something *cannot* come to be unless it enters into its limit or boundary; its boundary is its very *being*. In this sense, then, Athena does not cast a meditative look only upon that which is brought forth by humans, but more broadly – and "above all," Heidegger states – upon that which allows all things of the earth and sky that require *no* human action and production to come into their "limit" and therefore their being. This *that-by-which* all such beings come to be is what the ancient Greeks named *physis*. Again characteristically, he warns of the narrowing of the Greek understanding of *physis* in the Roman appropriation of *physis* as *natura*, but his central point is that the Greeks recognized (and therefore we may recognize once again) that *physis* is "that which emerges from itself forth into its respective limit and therein lingers" (138/121).[5]

Indeed, even today, he observes, "we are able to experience the fullness of the mystery of *physis* in Hellas, where in an astounding yet at the same time restrained manner there appears a mountain, an island, a coast, an olive tree." He admits that there is something to be said for the exceptional Greek visible "light" that allows us this experience, but this visible light is itself granted by another kind of light that is much more difficult to see (and for this reason is comparatively "invisible," which Athena, like the owl, is able to see). Yet before naming this unique light, he emphasizes that it was the Greeks who first recognized that *physis* – "the whole of the world" – always already addresses human beings and lays claim upon them so that human "knowing and doing" are compelled to correspond to this claim. Athena has her gleaming eyes upon *physis*, and as we know from the wealth of Heidegger's other reflections on the earliest Greek thinkers and poets, *physis* is another name for Being. Recall, for instance, his decisive statement in *Introduction to Metaphysics* (1935): "*Physis* is Being itself."[6] Accordingly, although he does not name Being in this address, we may say that it is Being as *physis* that ever rises up to us, opens us, and draws us into correspondence (*Entsprechung*). As I have expressed this in *Heidegger's Way of Being*: "*physis* endlessly arising and we endlessly astonished."[7]

Art, then, is a "correspondence" to and with *physis*, and this belonging together of *techne* and *physis* is but another way of characterizing the relation of the human being to Being. He returns to the primordial "light" by which and through which everything comes to be gathered into what it is. This is the "lightning-flash" (*der Blitz*) of which Heraclitus speaks in fragment 64: "But the lightning steers everything." The lightning brings everything into its "limit" and "steers" everything into place. From Heidegger's many other elucidations of this fragment we know that he reads this "lightning-flash" as another name for Being as "the primordial *Logos*" that lets be and gathers all that is, but here he does not restate this. He simply observes that the lightning is hurled by Zeus, "the highest god," and that Athena is Zeus's daughter. Athena alone knows where the lightning is kept, as she herself tells us in Aeschylus's *Eumenides*. Heidegger sums up by observing that it is precisely because Athena has this "knowing" that she is the manifold counselor, *polumetis*; the brightly seeing one, *glaucopis*; and the goddess who meditates on *physis*, *skeptomene*. We must hearken to Athena if we are "to understand even a little of the mystery of the provenance of art in Hellas."

II.   Opening to *Aletheia*: "Older" and "More Enduring" than the Human Being

What follows in the lecture is a disquisition on the perils of the contemporary age that is dominated by cybernetic and technological modeling and thinking. The age of unremitting calculative thinking has largely cut us off from that very "region" that is the provenance of art. The ground that he covers here is familiar; he had been making these same observations in much the same way throughout the 1960s.[8] This is not to say, of course, that the details of his critique in this particular lecture are not worth examining, yet I am more interested in distilling one crucial component of his critique to get to the heart of the matter.

To do this, let us restate in another way what we have already discussed. For Heidegger, *techne*, all human making, doing, and thinking – all human creation of whatever kind – emerges by virtue of our openness to that "region" in which all things emerge. We may call this "region," along with the ancient Greeks, *physis*. Our unfolding "belongs" with the unfolding of *physis*. We create along with *physis*. Our "artful" gathering corresponds with the primary gathering of *physis*. We might say, then, that our creation of any kind of "work" is always a "working with" Athena (or the other gods); that is, it is a "working with" *physis*, which Athena ever has her gleaming eyes upon. Ultimately, then, our "working with" entails that, on one level, we yield, give way, release ourselves to *physis*, which is beyond our making and control. So what, then, is the fundamental problem in the present age? If we distill Heidegger's message, it is this: The thoroughgoing *subjectivism* in the contemporary age has cut us off from our "source," *physis*. Two statements from his lecture bring this into sharpest relief:

> Industrial society constitutes the ultimate elevation of egoity [*Ichheit*], that is, of subjectivity. In it, the human being rests exclusively on itself and on the domains of its lived world, reworked into institutions.   (124/144)

> This is subjectivity resting only on itself. All objects are attributed to this subject. Industrial society arrogantly proclaims itself as the absolute norm of every objectivity.   (125/145)

At root, then, it is this conviction that we are the "source" of all that "is" that has so deformed and disabled us in the contemporary age by blocking us from entering into the fullness of our "essence" in relation to Being as *physis*. Heidegger specifically points to the dominance of "industrial society," but what he is assailing more generally is the insistence – embedded in our contemporary culture in manifold ways – that the human being measures out all that "is" and that "world" refers to no more than the sum of all human meaning and naming, interests and concerns, action and producing. We have become forgetful that any particular being (*ein Seiendes*) is always more than how it is measured out by the human being, and that Being itself (*Sein selbst*), the ontological temporal way or process wherein and whereby all beings issue forth, is always more than what the human being measures out as well. The contemporary insistence

on the human perspective is the chief impediment to our opening to Being as *physis* – as *Aletheia*.

Aletheia. Finally, we arrive at the other Greek *Ur*-word.
He calls upon us to take a "step-back" from the prevailing "egoity"
of the present age to enter again into the fullness of our existence. This means recovering and restoring our relation to "the
open and free domain" that bestows and grants all things, and
this domain was named by the Greeks "*A-letheia*." *A-letheia* or
"un-concealment" is the primordial "openness" that "does not
do away with concealment; rather unconcealment is invariably
in need of concealment" (127/147). He adds the hyphen in the
Greek word *A-letheia* to emphasize that the dimension of concealment and reserve – the *lethe* dimension – is intrinsic to all
revealing.

Yet we note, too, that he capitalizes the Greek word *Aletheia*,
as he had done on many occasions in his earlier work, and especially in the brilliant lecture courses on Parmenides, Heraclitus,
and Anaximander in the early 1940s.[9] In those places, Heidegger
repeatedly stated that *Aletheia* is another name for Being – and
we recognize this as his truly original and distinctive position
on "truth": "Truth" is in the first place the unending temporal
unfolding, the radiant emergence, of all that is. To put this succinctly, "is-ing" is "true-ing."[10] The capitalization of *Aletheia*
signals the continuity with the earlier work. *Aletheia* as Being
(Being as *Aletheia*) is the "open and free" domain or region that
grants all unconcealment and yet also holds back in reserve. *Aletheia* as Being is, in the first place, the locus of unconcealment
and concealment – *not the human being*, whatever our own activity of unconcealing and concealing.

This tells us most clearly that all persisting philosophical positions that posit the human being as the "source" of Being – that
is, as the "source" of all unconcealment and concealment – are
simply symptomatic of the hubris and narcissism of the prevailing modern subjectivism that the later Heidegger identified
again and again as blocking us from entering into the fullness of
our *Dasein*.[11]

The Greeks glimpsed the "region" that bestows all things,
including human beings and their "art," and they gave the name

aletheia (*A-letheia*) to this region – but also *physis*, provided that we keep in view the originary indication of this word. That is, insofar as *physis* names only the pure "light" or pure transparency of unconcealment as it came to be understood among the Greek philosophers (Plato's *eidos* or Aristotle's *morphe*, for example), then this name is not yet fundamental. Nevertheless, the earliest Greek thinkers and poets, and especially Heraclitus, had in view *physis* in the richest and fullest sense as the unending temporal emergence from concealment that ever shelters concealment. Heidegger cites Heraclitus's fragment 123, as he had so many times before, *physis kryptesthai philei*, or as he translates this saying here: "To emerging forth from itself, self-concealing properly belongs." What Heraclitus already knew we are called upon to know – and experience – once again for ourselves in the present age.

With a series of concluding questions, Heidegger makes the point that for us to restore and embrace our relation with (Being as *physis* as) *Aletheia* is for us to experience once again "awe" and "wonder" and "humility" (all translations of *Scheu*) before the unending temporal-spatial unfolding of all things and what "cannot be planned or controlled, or calculated and made" by us. In other words, our releasement to Being is a releasement from our subjectivist prisons, and this holds out the promise of our "dwelling" once more, of our finding our home again "upon the earth." A dwelling and abiding, he says, that is once again open to listening to "the voice" (*Stimme*) of *A-letheia*.[12] An openness that is not necessarily opposed to ontic mastering, but rather an openness, a releasement, that tempers and keeps humble these ontic efforts. He adds that while we do not know what will become of the present age, we do know that:

> the *A-letheia* that conceals itself in the Greek light, and which grants this light in the first place, *is older and more primordial and consequently more enduring* than every work and fabrication devised by human beings and brought forth by the human hand.
>
> (128/149; my italics)

This is the culminating statement. He maintains that *A-letheia* grants the Greek light in the first place. What does this mean?

He appears to be speaking of the "Greek light" of sheer unconcealment (*eidos, idea, morphe*), which was the focus of Plato and
Aristotle and the later medieval metaphysicians (*essentia, quidditas, actualitas*). Yet recall that the primordial light of *A-letheia* (as
unconcealment-concealment) was indeed glimpsed by the earliest Greek thinkers Parmenides, Anaximander, and Heraclitus; it
is the "lightning" of Zeus that grants and "steers" all things, the
"lightning" that is intimately known by Athena.

Yet to the crucial part of the line: *A-letheia* is "older, more primordial, and consequently more enduring" than the human
being and the full spectrum of "art." *A-letheia*, this ancient Greek
Ur-word for Being, is not dependent upon the human being.
Being as *A-letheia* is *independent* of the human being; that is, the
"is-ing" of all things unfolds both before and after the human
being, or along with the human being, but never dependent
upon the human being. The later Heidegger made this point in
several places, not simply in this lecture, and it captures the fundamental thrust of his thinking after *Being and Time*.[13]

Thus, what is at issue here is not the correlation of Being and
the human being in the expanse of the duration of human beings;
indeed, Heidegger always highlighted this correlation. What is
at issue, and what he is repudiating in this talk (and elsewhere
in the later work), is any human-centric position – including a
strict transcendental-phenomenological position – that holds
that Being "is" only insofar as the human being is. To put this
more pointedly: The later Heidegger is *not* a phenomenologist
in this strict sense. Indeed, it is any understanding of the "correlation" *that makes Being dependent upon the human being* that is
ruled out by his statement – and it must be ruled out if we are to
take a step in thinking toward breaking free of the prevailing and
unrelenting "egoity" or "subjectivism" that has taken hold of the
modern and contemporary age and that has installed the human
being as the measure of all things. We are called to recall, as he
states in another place, that "[Being as] *kosmos* is the measure-
giving; the measure that *kosmos* gives is it itself as *physis*."[14]

Being (as *physis* as *aletheia* as *kosmos*) is the "measure" that is
not made by us, and Heidegger is perfectly clear about this: "It
[Being itself (*Sein selbst*)] is nothing made and has therefore also

no determinate beginning at a point in time and no corresponding ending of its existence."[15] Yet this is so hard for us to understand and accept in the contemporary age – except most notably
in the *best* thinking of theoretical physics and science (which cannot be dismissed as mere "scientism"). It is possible, then, for us
to consider (even if Heidegger did not) that his later thinking
joins the deepest reflections of theoretical science in setting all
things free from our measure.

So, what is one compelling reason to continue to meditate on
Heidegger's thought? No small matter: to free all things from
ourselves. To free us from ourselves.

5 *Mythos*, Being, and the Appropriation of a Religious Tradition

Twentieth-century philosophical discourse was much concerned with the matter of myth. Ernst Cassirer, Karl Jaspers, and Paul Ricoeur were only some of the notable philosophers who attempted to discuss philosophically the myths – including the properly religious myths – of different peoples. Interestingly, though, Heidegger had little to say about myth, and, perhaps even more surprisingly, little scholarly attention has been paid to the few places in his work where he does, directly or indirectly, address this issue. The task here is to shed some light on Heidegger's understanding of myth and, further, to suggest a distinctively Heideggerian perspective on the appropriation of the mythology that is at the foundation of a religious tradition.

In the essay, "*Logos* (Heraclitus, Fragment B 50)," Heidegger approaches the problem of mythical language indirectly, yet his position appears to emerge quite clearly.[1] In the general discussion, he meditates on the Being-way as the *Logos*, "the laying that gathers." He maintains that the original meaning of the Greek word *legein* is "to lay and gather" or "to gatheringly let-lie-forth." By the name *Logos*, then, the Greeks named Being as the primordial *legein* that gatheringly lets-lie-forth all beings (including human beings). At one point, Heidegger pauses to consider and comment on another and, in his view, related Heraclitean fragment: "The One, which alone is wise, does not want and yet does want to be called by the name Zeus" (Diels-Kranz, B32).[2]

He begins by giving a highly novel interpretation of what the Greeks meant by the expression *Hen-Panta* (he capitalizes the Greek words), the One and the Many. According to Heidegger, *Hen-Panta* names Being as the *Logos* as the primordial laying-that-gathers. "*Hen-Panta* is not *what* the *Logos* pronounces," he states, "rather, *Hen-Panta* suggests the way in which *Logos* essentially occurs." In other words, *Hen-Panta* names Being as the temporal unfolding that lets all beings be: *Hen* names the One as Being as the unfolding itself by which and through which all beings are let be, and *Panta* names the ensemble of beings that are let be by the One as the unifying, gathering, assembling "way."

This clarified, he considers the fragment: "The One ... does not want to be called by the name of Zeus." His reading is that the Being-way, the *Hen*, the *Logos*, "is not in its innermost essence ready to appear under the name 'Zeus.'" The reason for this is that the name "Zeus" names "one present being among others," albeit "the highest of present beings," but Being cannot, in the first place, be named as a being, even as the highest being. "Zeus is not himself the *Hen*," Heidegger insists, because the *Hen* names not a being but the temporalizing Being-way that lets all beings be, including "Zeus," the highest being. Consequently, the originary *Hen* (the primordial *Logos*, Being) resists, in the first place, being named as *a being, even as the highest being*.

However, the fragment also states that the One "yet does want to be called by the name of Zeus." Heidegger understands this to mean that if we regard Being not as unfolding as such but as *what* has emerged into presence (the ensemble of *beings*, the *Panta*), then it is appropriate to name the One as Zeus as the highest being that comes to presence. He puts it clearly: "If Being is considered as the *Panta*, then and only then does the totality of present beings show itself under the direction of the highest present being as one totality under this One. The totality of present beings is under its highest aspect the *Hen* as Zeus." Therefore, the name Zeus names the One, not as the emerging and unfolding way, but as the highest present being among the total ensemble of beings that have come to presence (*Panta*). Although the name Zeus is distinctive insofar as it names the highest present being to which all other beings are ordered, still, the name

Zeus does *not* name Being as such, for Being, the *Logos*, the *Hen* is the very way by which Zeus, the highest present being, comes to presence.

Heidegger's discussion suggests several interesting conclusions. First, implicit in his argument is the position that the emergent highest present being has many different names; the highest being may be named Zeus or Allah – or Yahweh. Every historical people names this presencing supreme being uniquely.

Second, the name of this supreme being, including the name Yahweh, does *not* name Being as such. Indeed, his discussion seems to suggest that such *mythical naming* tends to hide or conceal or cover over the unfolding way as such. The powerful beauty and brilliance of mythical names may seduce us into forgetting the temporalizing Being-way, which is the very condition of the possibility of the appearing of the "gods." It is this forgetfulness of Being that leads us to speak of the emergent supreme being as "infinite" and "timeless." Yet to remain mindful of Being is to remain mindful that the name of the supreme being is limited to a particular historical showing of Being and that the highest present being itself, far from a timelessly enduring entity, is only a relatively more "abiding" presence.[3]

The third point follows from this. It seems that, for Heidegger, mythical utterance is not foundational utterance about Being. Mythical utterance names the gods – beings – and not Being, the unfolding way. What is more, the very resonance and power of the names of the gods tends to hold us fast and inclines us toward forgetfulness of the temporal and historical presencing of all beings, including the gods.

Heidegger's most explicit and extended discussion of the nature of myth may be found in his 1942/43 lecture course on Parmenides, which was published in German (1982). For our purposes, the critical text is Part I, section 6, part 2(f).[4] Here, Heidegger observes that there is more than simply a "phonetic designation" between the Greek words *theion*, "the divine" (*das Gotthafte*), and *theaon*, "the looking-beholding and shining-within" (*das Blickende and Hereinscheinende*). He reminds us that "the name as the first word is that which lets shine forth that which is to be named as it comes to presence in an originary way." Thus, insofar as by naming, a being is "nominated" as what it is, the similarity of the words *theion* and *theaon* suggests to Heidegger that what has been made manifest by the name in each case is fundamentally related.

Before pointing out what that fundamental relation is, he restates another basic position. It is human Dasein "who has the word." That is, it is the human being who, through the word, through naming, allows to come to presence in a distinctive manner what emerges into presence. Being may be "needless" in itself, but in this sense, Being "needs" human Dasein. That is, this particular linguistic disclosure of Being is brought to fulfillment by the human being "who has the word."

This said, Heidegger makes clear what the fundamental relation is between the Greek words *theion* and *theaon*: Being, as it "looks in and shines forth" (*theaon*),[5] was named by the Greeks *to theion*, or, as he says, "the gods" (*die Götter*). In other words, Being "looks in and shines forth" *as beings*, and such emergent beings (the "highest" beings) were named by the Greeks "the gods." This particular manner of naming beings he calls *mythos*: "The word, as the naming of Being, *mythos*, names Being in its originary looking-in and shining forth; it names *to theion*, that is, the gods." Thus, "the gods" is the properly *mythical* word with which the human being makes manifest what emerges into manifestation.

This mythical naming, the naming of the gods, he characterizes as "the appropriate mode of the relation [of the human being] to Being as it shines forth." We may understand him to mean that *mythos*, the naming of the gods, is a *proper* correspondence of human Dasein to Being as it shines forth. Indeed, unlike in the essay on the *Logos*, he goes on to suggest in this section that *mythos* is, at least in one respect, foundational utterance. The *Gottsager*, the one who names the gods, experiences the gods coming forth in all their resplendence and awe-fulness, and thus the *Gottsager* at least *implicitly* recognizes Being as emergence.[6]

Only when Being is no longer experienced as *aletheia*, emergence as such, he continues, does the naming of the gods, *mythos*, become unnecessary and irrelevant. In typically provocative fashion, he argues that the loss of the gods (*Götter-losigkeit*) in the contemporary period – a-theism (*A-theismus*) – is not to be traced to the proud and irresponsible thinking of modern philosophers. The principal source of the prevailing god(s)-lessness is (substance) metaphysics. The gods already ceased to "shine forth" in the metaphysics of the tradition that conceived them to be beings among beings that are merely there. Already in classical substance metaphysics, which no longer thought Being as the process of emergence, *mythos*, the task of *naming* the gods, became essentially unnecessary and irrelevant.

This is all debatable, of course, but in any case, in the Parmenides text, Heidegger is quite clear that *mythos* is an appropriate – and indeed necessary – mode of correlation of human Dasein with Being. Consequently, *mythos* is a more foundational or originary utterance than traditional metaphysical expressions of substance and essence. Even so, in this same section, he adds the crucial observation that even "the essence of the divinity" is "dominated from the very beginning" by Being as *aletheia*. This remark cautions us: The naming of the gods, *mythos*, is unique and privileged utterance insofar as it "shines forth" Being "*in its originary looking-in and shining forth*," that is, insofar as it makes manifest beings (the highest beings) that emerge and abide. Yet such naming, strictly speaking, does not name Being itself, the unfolding way.

It seems, then, that Heidegger also wishes to maintain that mythical utterance is not foundational utterance in the fullest sense because it makes manifest principally beings (even the highest beings) and not Being, the way by which all beings – including the "gods" – emerge. Finally, then, the Parmenides text and the essay on the *Logos* appear to converge on this point: *mythos* calls forth principally the gods – beings – which emerge and thus leaves essentially unilluminated the very ontological "way" by which such beings emerge in the first place. And since Heidegger's singular concern was precisely with the *letting be* of beings, it becomes more clear why he was not so very much concerned with the issue of *mythos* in his writings.

These two texts, then, which were conceived at approximately the same time, tell us a great deal about Heidegger's fundamental understanding of the nature of mythical utterance. For Heidegger, the god(s) and the stories of the god(s) – which form the basis of every religious tradition – must be understood in the light of the understanding of the Being-way. More specifically, this means that the being of the god may be thought only within the horizon of time and history. In the first place, the god, the supreme being, is thinkable, not as an immutable and timeless entity, but, rather, as a relatively perduring emergence; the god "abides" or "whiles." Secondly, the "abiding" or "whiling" god is named differently in different epochs. The "abiding" god has many different names.

In texts such as this at least, it seems that Heidegger leaves open only this possibility for the appropriation of a religious tradition – and specifically, it would seem that he leaves open only this possibility for the appropriation of the Judeo-Christian tradition. Indeed, in the Parmenides text, he explicitly criticizes Christian belief for its forgetfulness of the Being-way.[7] He argues that the ancient Greeks remained mindful of the emerging of the gods to the extent that they acknowledged that the gods – and even the highest god, Zeus – were subject to *moira*. Yet this mindfulness of the emerging of the gods – present in some way in the time of the Greeks – was lost in the epoch of Christianity. The Christian God, he ruefully observes, is the master of being, but the "gods of the Greeks," he continues, "are not 'personalities' and 'persons' who master Being, but are beings through which Being itself looks in."

Consequently, as Heidegger appears to see it, the traditional Christian understanding of the human being's relationship to God must be reinterpreted in the light of the retrieval of the classical metaphysical understanding of Being. The Judeo-Christian *mythos* – powerful and resonant in itself – must, nevertheless, be *re-appropriated* in accordance with the understanding of Being as the temporal way. In effect, this means that one is called upon to remain mindful that the God of Abraham, Isaac, and Jacob, no less than the supreme deity of every religious tradition, is not the master of Being, but a being, albeit the highest being, through which Being itself looks in and shines forth.

Nevertheless, we must keep in mind that this is not Heidegger's only word or final word on the matter of "God" and "the divine," as I point out in later reflections in this book.[8] It is but one perspective, and no doubt a provocative and debatable perspective, suggested by Heidegger's commentaries over the course of his long lifetime of thinking.

6 On Heidegger's Heraclitus Lectures: In Nearness of a Process Metaphysics?

For Beyng is everlasting, but also on the way into its own truth.

Heidegger, 1944 Heraclitus Lecture Course (GA 55: 345)

Heidegger's sparkling lecture courses on Heraclitus from 1943 and 1944 were published in his *Collected Works* (*Gesamtausgabe*) in 1979 as Volume 55 (GA 55, edited by the late Manfred Frings), but, unfortunately, they have been largely overlooked in the Heidegger scholarship.[1] It is arguable that the core of the later Heidegger's thinking on "Being" may be found in his commentaries on Parmenides, Heraclitus, and Anaximander from his extraordinarily creative period of the 1940s. Admittedly, his readings of these earliest Greek thinkers are highly speculative – and they continue to provoke scholarly challenges – yet what is undeniable is their originality and brilliance. Heidegger found in the fragments of these early thinkers a manifold of "names" for Being itself (*Sein selbst*): *physis, alētheia, zoē, hen, kosmos, apeiron*, the primordial *Logos*, and so forth.

For Heidegger, each of these Greek *Ur*-words named the earliest and most fundamental Western understanding of "Being" as the unitary temporal unfolding of all things, that is, Being-as-time or, as I prefer to say, the "Being-way." As he saw it, this originary understanding of Being was later eclipsed or "forgotten" as Western thinking devolved into a thinking of "being" principally in terms of the timeless and changeless, namely, as *eidos idea, morphē, essentia, essence.* Thus, in his view, the urgent "task" for thinking in the present day is to recall and recover the earliest Greek experience and thinking of Being and thereby to rename it in a new and refreshed manner; hence, also his own terms of art, *Ereignis, Lichtung,* and *Es gibt,* all names for Being itself.

These lecture courses are brimming with engaging reflections on the meaning and significance of the fragments of Heraclitus. In the 1943 lecture course, Heidegger unfolds at length how *physis* was but another name for "Being" (the Greek word *einai* and the word *on* in its participial form and verbal sense). Heraclitus and the earliest Greeks experienced *physis* as Being as "the pure emerging," and for them, all beings and things – "mountain and sea, plant and animal, houses and human beings, gods and heaven" (102) – emerged from out of this pure emerging. Furthermore, the Greeks experienced *everything* as "living" (*zoē*) insofar as everything emerges from out of the pure emerging itself. And since this pure emerging or unconcealing was also named by the Greeks as *alētheia,* the Greek *Ur*-words *physis, zoē, alētheia* all say "the Same" (*das Selbe*) and illuminate, each name in a somewhat different manner, Being itself.

Heidegger continues with a long excursus (128ff.) on Heraclitus's fragment 123 (*physis kryptesthai philei,* traditionally translated into English as "Nature loves to hide"), and he offers his distinctive reading that being as *physis* as *alētheia* is never fully transparent to us. All emergence is fraught with "concealment," which is his signature way of saying that the emergence and shining forth of things is never exhausted by our thinking and saying, our sense or meaning. "Concealment" is the unconquerable reserve of Being that was brought to language by the earliest Greeks in the *lēthe* of *alētheia* and the *kryptesthai* of Heraclitus's fragment 123.

Also notable in this lecture course is his extended poetic philosophical reflection (161ff.) on Being as the "fire" (*pur*) that allows all beings to flame up in the first place, and as the "lightning flash" (*keraunos*) that "steers" all beings into their proper place and relation. According to Heidegger, Heraclitus is always drawing our attention to that which *enables* all beings to be as they are, and as they are in relation to one another in the ensemble. The focus is away from beings or even beings as a whole, and toward Being as the "inapparent harmony" (*harmonia aphanes*) that "shimmers ungraspably" through all beings as they emerge and unfold. This emerging and unfolding is the shining way of all beings, and this was also named by Heraclitus as *kosmos*. *Kosmos*, too, is a name for Being.

Being as *physis* as *kosmos* is, as Heidegger reads Heraclitus, the "primordial emblazoning and adorning" (*das ursprüngliche Schmücken und Zieren*) that brings all beings into their radiant existence, and I discussed this distinctive motif in detail in Chapter 1. Yet to gloss the matter more plainly here: Heidegger's distinction between the "apparent harmony" of all beings and the "inapparent harmony" of Being (as *physis* as *kosmos*) is a reminder of his life-long concern with the "ontological difference," or simply the "difference" (*Unterschied*), between Being and beings.

Furthermore, this "difference" cannot be explained away, as some commentators are inclined to do, as an epistemological or transcendental-phenomenological difference between the structural conditions of knowing and the objects of knowing thus constituted. Heidegger repeatedly makes statements that point to the "metaphysical" (indeed, "ontological") character of this difference. So, for example, he emphasizes the wisdom of Heraclitus's teaching in fragment 30 that "none of the gods, as well as no one of the human beings" has brought forth Being as *kosmos*. He adds: "It [Being] is nothing made and has therefore also no determinate beginning at a point in time and no corresponding ending of its existence." Moreover, in the second lecture course, he states that Being (written in this instance as *Seyn*, "Beyng") is "everlasting, but also on the way into its own truth" (345).

In the 1944 lecture course, Heidegger turned his attention to Heraclitus's "teaching" (*Lehre*, often mistranslated in Heidegger studies as "doctrine") on "*logos*," and his overarching concern was to affirm the primacy of Being as "the primordial *Logos*" (Heidegger used the capital *lamda* when referring to Being) in "relation" to the *logos* (*legein*) of the human being. Being as the primordial *Logos* is the temporal "laying out" and "fore-gathering" of all things that is always prior to and exceeds any distinctively human "gathering" in language or art. He is explicit and emphatic that being as "the primordial *Logos*" is "indeed a kind of saying and word" (259) and also "a kind of speech and voice" (244) – but certainly not "any kind of activity of human saying or stating" (277). The primordial *Logos* is "expressly not the voice of a human being" (244), he maintains. Our human task is to "hearken" in humble silence to what the primordial *Logos* "says" and respond in word and art, and this is the teaching of Heraclitus on the unique *homologein*, or "correspondence" (*Entsprechung*), of human beings in relation to the *Logos*.

There are other striking readings and tropes in both lecture courses that have gone largely unnoticed in the Heidegger scholarship, but which I discuss in greater detail in *Heidegger's Way of Being* and also in Chapter 1 of the present volume.[2] Yet the central issue I raise here is that this volume on Heraclitus, along with other major texts from the later years, presents a major challenge to certain contemporary readings of Heidegger: namely, it puts into radical question the currently oft-repeated claim that Heidegger "overcame" metaphysics. Although it is true that his reflections in these lecture courses bear out that he sought to move beyond a metaphysics and theology of *substance or essence*, nonetheless, at the same time, they also suggest an alternatively conceived metaphysical and religious or spiritual perspective.

As we have observed, his discussion of Being as *physis* as *kosmos* bears all the marks of a distinctive metaphysical position: Being as radiant, "everlasting," temporal unfolding that is "on its way into its own truth" and by which, in which, and through which all particular beings are related and emerge into their own truth, linger, and pass away. Is this not a "process" metaphysics of some kind? It would seem so, but Heidegger does not tell us as much, unlike Alfred North Whitehead, for example. Still, the later Heidegger was always leaning and pressing in this direction. In the 1944 lecture course, we find him repeatedly seeking to redefine the "relation" of Being and the human being. He is clearly not satisfied with the traditional classical or medieval metaphysical account of this relation, yet at the same time, in some passages, he insists on the "independence" of Being in relation to the human being. In one such important text, he states:

> Being is in need of *legein*. Is Being thereby dependent upon the human being, if it is the case that *legein* is the "human" of the human being? Here remains to question: What does "dependence" mean here? Is this dependence a degradation of Being? What if Being were in need of *legein* since it, Being, is what is *independent*? What if this *independence* of Being consisted in the fact that Being is the originally sheltering, that is gleaning, that is gathering of everything – the *Logos*? Because Being is the *Logos*, it needs *legein*. [But] Being needs *legein* for the favor of the safeguarding of Being's *independence*. Here we are thinking in that region (in the region of the truth of Beyng) where all relations are entirely different than in the field of beings.
>
> (379; my italics for "independent" and "independence")

Thus, what we have here, too, is a sketch of a metaphysical (and even theological) position that Heidegger never worked out – or, rather, quite decidedly never wished to work out. Being is the unitary, temporal, dynamic unfolding process that is not "a being" and that is "independent" of the human being; yet Being is "related" to the human being (and to all beings, "everything"), but not as "a being" to another being in the realm of beings.

Admittedly, then, Heidegger was reluctant or unwilling to follow through on such novel metaphysical implications in his own later thinking on Being (Beyng), yet he nevertheless put into play again and again precisely these possibilities with his manifold characterizations and poetic descriptions of Being. These Heraclitus lectures are a perfect illustration of this tendency in his later thinking. We simply cannot overlook the fact that his readings of Heraclitus move in a nearness to a "process" metaphysical view of things along the lines of Whitehead and others. Thus, consider: For Heidegger, Being as *kosmos* as "the all-unifying One" (286) is the temporal, dynamic, creative unfolding of all beings; "beings" are temporal "events" (not timeless "substances") that are unfolded and enfolded by Being; Being is the "fire," the "shimmering *kosmos*," that is temporally "everlasting" and that is "on its way into its own truth," along with all beings, which, in turn, are related each to each and all to Being as "the all-unifying One." These parallels with a process metaphysics of some kind are evident, and in Part III, I offer yet another clue on thinking Heidegger and Whitehead together.

The key point is that there does appear to be a philosophical correspondence between the later Heidegger's thinking of Being and Whitehead's process metaphysics. I do not wish to claim too much, however, since Heidegger was constitutionally opposed to any kind of "systematic" thinking, and thus he did not elaborate his suggestive indications on Being and "the divine." He was content to point to these fundamental matters with the all the richness of language that he could muster, and in this way, he was a different kind of thinker from Whitehead (and from most in the Anglo-American tradition of philosophical thinking). Even so, most academic philosophers and students today know little or nothing about Whitehead, and so they would be quite surprised by the openness and creativity of his "metaphysical" language. Indeed, many Heidegger commentators would not expect that Whitehead – the "metaphysician" – was fully aware of the finitude, limitation, and tentativeness of all our descriptions of Being. As Whitehead put it in the Preface to his *Process and Reality* (1929): "how shallow, puny, and imperfect are efforts to sound the depths in the nature of things. In philosophical discussion, the merest hint of dogmatic certainty as to the finality of statement is an exhibition of folly."

It is also apparent that Heidegger was, from the outset of his path of thinking, aiming for a transformed thinking of Being and "the divine." His fundamental insight into Being-as-time ruled out any kind of traditional metaphysics or theology of timeless substances or essences (what he called "onto-theology"). Consequently, the ancient Catholic theology that he grew up with was unacceptable to him. Yet the drive or impulse to the divine remained prevalent in his thinking of Being, and his many mysterious poetic characterizations of Being in the Heraclitus lecture courses approximate a "process" divinity of some kind, perhaps similar to Whitehead's attempt at the conclusion of *Process and Reality* in the section "God and the World." Perhaps. In any case, what is undeniable is that Heidegger had an abiding "religious" or "spiritual" sense that something far greater than human beings (and greater than the whole ensemble of beings) was working itself out in time and that something extraordinary was "happening" (*Ereignis*) over time. We humans are only a part of this wondrous and mysterious unfolding. As he expressed this in the 1944 lecture course: Being as the *Logos* is "the all-unifying One" and "this is precisely what the human being must know: it is the to-be-thought that is before all else, in all else, and beyond all else" (286). How can commentators overlook or dismiss this kind of "metaphysical" language?

⁓⁓⁓⁓⁓

Heidegger's fascinating lecture courses on Heraclitus contribute to our understanding of the content and trajectory of his later thinking. They also remind us that Heidegger, despite his determination to "overcome" a traditional metaphysics of substance, was, nonetheless, always in some way *on the way* toward an alternative metaphysical understanding of "Being." His aim from the outset was a revised characterization of Being, and the fragments of the earliest Greek thinkers Heraclitus, Parmenides, and Anaximander constituted his royal road to that end. Admittedly, he left us only a sketch of this new (or renewed) understanding of Being, but that was entirely consistent with his hinting style and his aversion to any kind of systematic philosophical thinking. Almost fifty years after his death and after the publication of over one hundred volumes of his writings, it is evident that Heidegger's open-ended and suggestive style of thinking has led to many different readings and appropriations. Yet it is also undeniable that there is the Heidegger whose inkling was not to "overcome" metaphysics as such, but rather to *refashion* it along the lines of his creative and distinctive vision of Being.

7 The Path through Heidegger's Thought

An Interview with Prof. Vladimír Leško for *FILOZOFIA*[1]

You are well-known in Slovakia as a philosopher and the author of two original books about Heidegger´s philosophy, Engaging Heidegger *and* Heidegger's Way of Being. *For a long time you have conducted research on Heidegger´s work, but we know that you started with the study of Economics at the university and not philosophy. We are interested to know what prompted this change in direction.*

First, my heartfelt thanks to you and to your colleagues for your generous interest in my work on Heidegger. I am delighted to hear of this, and I extend my greetings and good wishes to your philosophical community in Slovakia.

Yes, it is true that my first studies were in Economics, and I remain very much interested in the history of economic ideas. Yet I also discovered in myself a concern for investigating even more fundamental issues about being human and about our existence and our reality. This led me to the study of philosophy, and I considered all the great ancient Greek thinkers. There is such profound wisdom in ancient Greek philosophy (and in classical philosophy generally), and to this day I continue to read and study and teach these remarkable works.

As I advanced in my philosophical studies and concerned myself with all the other great philosophers in the history of philosophy, I also attended lectures by Hans-Georg Gadamer when he visited in the United States, and I recall that he spoke so glowingly about how Heidegger was such a dynamic and engaging teacher. Heidegger, he would say, brought ancient Greek philosophy alive in a new way. Heidegger wanted to dig down past all the tired and worn propositions that were handed down about ancient Greek thinking in order to unearth the living "root" experiences that were the *source* of their thinking and their terminology – and, indeed, these experiences are the source of all philosophical thinking. I recall being excited all over again to study Greek philosophy, and I immersed myself in the study of Heidegger's writings. With the guidance of the preeminent Heidegger commentator of the day, William J. Richardson, I engaged all that Heidegger had to say, and I was amazed at the richness of his thinking. Heidegger breathed life into the study of philosophy; he made it living and fresh. And after all these many years, I continue to try to approach my own teaching and writing in this same way. I wish for my students and for readers of my work to be brought into the "experiences" that flow into philosophical reflection, and not simply to memorize and recite "positions" and "propositions."

So, to come back to your question, I think that there is, of course, great value in the study of all the academic disciplines, but when one is led to ask the deepest questions, one is led to the study of philosophy.

Your philosophy studies are closely associated with Boston College and your professor and mentor William J. Richardson, who wrote the important book Heidegger: Through Phenomenology to Thought. *Would you please tell us something about him and the importance of his research for us today?*

William J. Richardson was my teacher and mentor, and in the later years, he was a friend and colleague. In the last decade, I was delighted to give presentations with him, and I was honored that he provided a Foreword to my first book *Engaging Heidegger*. Recently, he passed away at the age of 96, and Heidegger studies lost a true giant. But he lived a full and rich life, and his work on Heidegger will continue to influence future generations of students of Heidegger's thinking.

Prof. Richardson's great book, *Heidegger: Through Phenomenology to Thought*, was first published in 1963, and it brought into view the centrality of the *Seinsfrage* in Heidegger's lifetime of thinking. My own work continues and extends in new ways his foundational research. Yet on a personal note, Bill (as I knew him) told wonderful stories about the research and writing of his book, and especially about his decisive meeting with Heidegger in 1959. In my conversations with Bill right up to the very end of his life, he always recalled Heidegger's graciousness, and he remained struck at how profoundly calm and meditative Heidegger became when he looked out into the wooded landscape from the window of his study in Zähringen. Heidegger took on the countenance of a "nature mystic," he would say to me.

The importance of Prof. Richardson's book remains insofar as he showed, with such philosophical rigor and clarity, how Heidegger unfolded the core matter of Being over his whole lifetime of thinking.

In 2011, when I began reading your book Engaging Heidegger, *I was struck by how Prof. Richardson had praise for your studies [in the Foreword]. I agreed with the three things that he highlighted about your book. Would you present to our readers who have not read your book yet how you see the essence of Heidegger's "engaging" thinking?*

My first book, *Engaging Heidegger*, was an effort to show the centrality of the Being-question in the whole of Heidegger's work, but I wanted to use texts that had not been carefully considered in the scholarship thus far, for example, the *Four Seminars* (*Vier Seminare*) that Heidegger conducted for French colleagues in the years 1966–73. My discussion of the *Four Seminars*, which forms the heart of Chapter 1, shows clearly that the later Heidegger remained focused on the matter of Being right to the very end of his life. In Chapter 2, I considered both his early *Ereignis*-writings and the later *Ereignis*-writings to make clear that Heidegger thought of his distinctive term, *Ereignis*, as another name for Being itself (*Sein selbst*). And this is also true for his other original term, *Lichtung*, which is the topic of both Chapters 5 and 6. These chapters bring into view what had not been clarified before in the scholarship: that Being remained Heidegger's principal concern and that his terms of art, *Ereignis* and *Lichtung*, are other names for Being. In other words, these terms say "the Same" (*das Selbe*) to use his language, but they are not simply "identical" in an empty, logical sense.

Engaging Heidegger is also centrally concerned with the relation of the human being to Being, and through careful textual analysis I highlight how the early Heidegger is quite different from the later Heidegger in characterizing this relation existentially. Chapters 3 and 4 chart the movement in his thinking from emphasizing the mood of *Angst* to the mood of "astonishment," and from the theme of our "homelessness" to our "being-at-home" in relation to Being. This kind of thorough analysis of the development of Heidegger's thinking on these issues had never been taken up in the scholarship beforehand.

Finally, *Engaging Heidegger* seeks to highlight the beauty and resonance of Heidegger's thinking. Heidegger was arguably the most "engaging" philosopher of the twentieth century, and I wanted to help make that clear by "engaging" his thinking in a careful and rigorous way – but also in a lively and "engaging" manner. And I hope readers agree.

For the moment, let us stay with Engaging Heidegger. *In this book you emphasize Heidegger's teaching in the context of his four seminars with his French colleagues – in* Le Thor *(1966, 1968, 1969) and in* Zähringen *(1973). You propose that Heidegger's later thought is a reaffirmation of the beginning of his Denkweg. For our readers, could you summarize this point?*

Some recent Heidegger commentators have argued that Heidegger neglected the *Seinsfrage* in the later years, but the *Four Seminars* confirm that the Being-question remained central to his thinking to the very end. In the last seminar in 1973 in Zähringen, it is stated clearly and decisively that "We must emphasize again and again that the only question that has ever moved Heidegger is the question of Being: What does Being mean?"

Thus, in *Engaging Heidegger*, I show how in each of the many seminars over the years 1966 to 1973, Heidegger returned again and again to clarifying the fundamental features of Being. In addition, Being – understood as the temporal-spatial emerging and unfolding of all beings – is also named *physis, aletheia*, the primordial *Logos, kosmos, Ereignis*, and *Lichtung*. Heidegger had maintained this position for many years, as I have also shown in my second book, *Heidegger's Way of Being*, but in the *Four Seminars* he affirmed his readings once again. I also quote from a letter that Heidegger wrote to Manfred Frings in 1966: "For it is this question of Being – and it alone – that determines the way of my thought and its boundaries."

In the last seminar in 1973, Heidegger offered an important reading about Parmenides. How do you understand its importance?

As you observe, in the last seminar in Zähringen in 1973, Heidegger read a short statement on Parmenides that we may say sums up his lifetime of thinking about Being. What I note, however, is that his final statement on Parmenides is similar to the many other statements that he had composed over the whole course of his lifetime. In particular, Heidegger's statement recalls his reading of the fragments of Parmenides in his 1951–2 lecture course *What is Called Thinking? (Was heißt Denken?)*. At the heart of Heidegger's reflection is his effort to elucidate fragment 6 that calls upon us to say and take to heart "*eon: emmenai*" (the archaic Greek spelling of "*on: einai*").

As Heidegger worked this out, Parmenides, at the very dawn of Western thinking, gave us to think Being as the one fundamental "way" (the Being-way, as I prefer to name it) that unfolds all beings. In other words, "*eon: emmenai*" means *the emergent being (eon) in its very emerging (emmenai)*. Or to put this another way, it refers to that-which-is present (*das Anwesende*) in its very presencing (*anwesen selbst*). Admittedly, Heidegger's elucidation of the fragment is dense and difficult, but his meaning is apparent enough: to meditate on Being is to meditate on the temporal dynamic process whereby and wherein all beings issue forth and come to be, that is, the emerging of all that emerges.

In your work, you write at length and cogently about how Heidegger's understanding of Being (Sein) needs to be carefully clarified. On the one hand, there is the beingness of beings, but his emphasis was always on recovering an understanding of Being itself (das Sein selbst; das Sein als solches; das Sein als Sein) – Being considered, as he sometimes said, without regard to beings. Could you say more about Being itself in this way? Is it possible to "know" Being itself?

Your question goes to the heart of a clarification that must be made in order to understand Heidegger's original and distinctive thinking about Being, and it is a clarification that I seek to make in both of my books. What we may glean from his life-long reflections and meditations is that Being itself or Beyng (*Sein selbst/Seyn*) lets beings (*das Seiende*) be in their beingness (*die Seiendheit*). As he put this simply and elegantly in 1945: "Now Beyng is that which lets each and every being be what it is and how it is, precisely because Beyng is the freeing that lets every single thing rest in its abiding fullness; that is, Beyng safeguards each and every thing." In other words, Being, which is not a particular being, is the temporal-spatial ontological "way" whereby and wherein all beings issue forth, come to be, in their beingness (*Seiendheit*), that is, in their full appearance or "full look" (the ancient Greek philosophical terms *eidos*, *morphe* and the medieval terms *essentia*, *quidditas*). Being is the pure emerging of all that emerges (*physis*). Being is the pure manifesting of all that is manifest (*aletheia*). Being is the pure laying-out and gathering of all that is (the primordial *Logos*). This understanding of Being, although already in evidence in the early work, came into fullest view in his "later" writings and reflections. So, yes, indeed, "knowing" Being is possible, but we do not know – and say – Being in the same way that we know and say beings; and that is the challenge.

Some researchers, such as Otto Pöggeler, think that Heidegger's second most important work is Contributions to Philosophy (From Ereignis). *I was very pleased when I read in both of your books that you consider Heidegger's most important work in the 1930s to be*

Introduction to Metaphysics *(1935). What is your thinking about* Contributions *in relation to* Introduction to Metaphysics?

It is true that in recent years, Heidegger's private manuscript *Beiträge* or *Contributions to Philosophy (From Ereignis)*, which he composed between 1936 and 1938, has become the focal point of a number of Heidegger commentators. This may be understandable because this text was not published until after Heidegger's death, and it is a very enigmatic work. Some of the scholarship has been superb, but some commentators wish to see in this text the promise of getting to some "secret" teaching of Heidegger or of getting to the *Ur*-Heidegger that somehow unlocks the meaning of all his other writings – and neither is the case in my view.

More simply, this manuscript represents Heidegger's experimental efforts in the 1930s to revise and restate his core concerns. It is a notable work because it gives us a vivid picture of Heidegger wrestling with language to say in a fresh way the basic themes of his thinking, especially as he was making the transition to his later work. Yet we must not overstate the importance of this text. From the longer perspective of Heidegger's place in the history of philosophy, I think that the two most important texts from the 1930s will be his *Introduction to Metaphysics* and his essay "The Origin of the Work of Art." As I point out in Chapter 4 of *Heidegger's Way of Being*, Heidegger himself considered *Introduction to Metaphysics* to be one of his most important statements, and we must return to it if we are to understand and appreciate the core matter of his thinking – and communicate it clearly to others. *Introduction to Metaphysics* is a masterwork that is more accessible to a larger philosophical audience – now and in the future – than *Beiträge*.

Heidegger brings to the philosophy of the twentieth century many new philosophical ideas and terms, and two of the most important are die Lichtung and das Ereignis. You rightly pay great attention to them in your researches. How do you understand these terms, and how important is it that Heidegger states that "Die Lichtung selber aber is das Sein" ("But the clearing itself is Being")?

Heidegger loved language, and he was always trying to find new ways to bring to language the core matter that he had in view. His principal concern was with Being/Beyng, but he also found new and refreshed ways of saying this, and *Ereignis* and *Lichtung* are his own distinctive terms, his *terms of art*, if you will. In *Engaging Heidegger*, I examine Heidegger's understanding of *Lichtung* in Chapters 5 and 6, which represents a step forward in the scholarship, as you point out. There is so much to say about Heidegger's use of this term, but to answer your question more succinctly, it is clear that Heidegger understood *Lichtung* to be another name for Being/Beyng. As you note, he states this most decisively in the 1947 *Letter on Humanism*: "But the clearing itself is Being." What this means is that although there is a correlation between the human being and Being, it is Being that is the clearing or opening of all things in the first place. We human beings are able to "clear" or "open" things in language only because Being has cleared or opened all things – that is, allowed them to come to be – in the first place. Heidegger emphasized the priority and primacy of Being as "the clearing itself" (*die Lichtung selbst*) or as "the open itself" (*das Offene selbst*).

You ask in Chapter 2 of Engaging Heidegger: *what is the case with das Ereignis? How is it that Ereignis is (only) another name for Being itself?*

Some recent commentators have stated that Heidegger subordinated his notion of Being/Beyng to the notion of *Ereignis*, but I do not think that this is the case. In the early *Beiträge* and the *Beiträge*-related manuscripts, he often states that "*Ereignis* is Beyng" or that "Beyng is *Ereignis*," and he also frequently cites "Beyng as *Ereignis*" or "*Ereignis* as Beyng." This is also the case in his later *Ereignis*-writings of the late 1950s and early 1960s. Most notably, in his famous 1962 lecture "Time and Being," he brings his remarks on *Ereignis* to a conclusion by stating that "the sole aim of this lecture has been to bring into view Being itself as *Ereignis*." In Chapter 2 of *Engaging Heidegger* and in other essays, I present all this textual evidence to show that Heidegger always considered his distinctive term *Ereignis* to be only another name for Being/Beyng. In other words, both names bring into view the core matter (*die Sache selbst*), but perhaps we can say that the word *Ereignis* is especially effective in bringing into view the temporal "happening" or "coming to pass" of all beings, including ourselves.

In Engaging Heidegger, *you give much attention to the investigation of Plato's understanding of "light" and Heidegger's phenomenon of "the clearing." How do you see the relation of Plato's understanding of light to the phenomenon of the clearing?*

Yes, both Chapters 5 and 6 of *Engaging Heidegger* are concerned with Heidegger's notion of *die Lichtung* and the long and interesting story of his engagement with Plato's metaphor of "light," especially as we find it in the "Allegory of the Cave" as told by Socrates in Bk. VII of the *Republic*. I also make mention of the medieval "metaphysics of light" as another source of inspiration for Heidegger.

One key issue is that in his multiple readings of Plato's "Allegory of the Cave," from 1926 to 1940, Heidegger does not read the light of the sun as "ontic" or as "onto-theological." Indeed, the sun, this "light-source" or "primordial light," as he puts it, is precisely what makes *possible* all that is lighted and therefore visible. In other words, for Heidegger, the sun, Plato's "symbol" for the Idea of the Good, is what enables/ lets through/ opens up/ frees up all beings and all ontic truth about beings – and this "letting" is the fundamental matter, *die Sache selbst*. In all these readings, therefore, Heidegger elucidated his own fundamental concern with Being – the letting be of beings in their beingness – in terms of the trope or theme of light that he appropriated from Plato. Although Heidegger regarded the *manifested* light as "ontic," this is not the case with respect to the *manifesting* light of the sun – which represents Being itself. Thus, this distinction between the manifesting/manifested light is the figurative equivalent of the "ontological difference" between Being and beings. The later Heidegger had a more ambivalent relationship with Plato's metaphor of "light," and I explore this matter further in both *Engaging Heidegger* and *Heidegger's Way of Being*.

The German thinker Günter Figal has given much attention to Hei-
degger's work on Aristotle. He has argued that Heidegger remained
an Aristotelian philosopher (Figal, G.: Heidegger als Aristoteliker. In:
Heidegger-Jahrbuch 3. Heidegger und Aristoteles. Hrsg. A. Denker,
G. Figal, F. Volpi, H. Zaborowski. München/Freiburg: Verlag Karl
Alber 2007, 53). I do not agree. It seems that Heidegger had interest
in Aristotle between 1922 and 1930, but that after that period he
turned his attention more and more to the pre-Platonic thinkers Par-
menides and Heraclitus. In Introduction to Metaphysics *(1935),*
Aristotle and Plato are less important than Parmenides and Heracli-
tus. What is your view on Heidegger and Aristotle?

This is a very complex question to answer in a short space.
To put it briefly, I do think that Aristotle played a crucial role in
Heidegger's whole lifetime of thinking, but I also agree with you
that Heidegger ultimately gave preeminent place to "the earliest
Greek thinkers" (the pre-Socratic thinkers) Anaximander, Par-
menides, and Heraclitus (as he understood them).

To me, the most important statement made by Heidegger on
Aristotle is his essay "On the Essence and Concept of *physis* in
Aristotle's *Physics* B, 1," which he composed in 1939 (but not
published until 1958). This essay goes well beyond his earlier
discussions of Aristotle in the 1920s, and it reflects his more fully
developed and mature understanding of Aristotle's thinking.
In particular, Heidegger illuminates Aristotle's fundamental
insight into the *temporal* character of Being (*kinesis*) and how, in
this way, Aristotle remained closer than Plato to the originary
understanding of Being in Anaximander, Parmenides, and Heraclitus. Heidegger never ceased admiring Aristotle's thinking, but
he also recognized that Aristotle also contributed to the devolution in the thinking of Being by shifting attention to the "timeless" "form" of things. Consequently, in this latter respect, we
can say, as you suggest, that, for Heidegger, the earliest Greek
thinkers (the pre-Socratics) remained more decisive for his thinking of Being than Aristotle.

In Engaging Heidegger *we find: "Heidegger meditated a lifetime*
on what was first named in the West by Parmenides and Hera-

clitus as eon – Being." The further development of this idea we find in your second book Heidegger's Way of Being. *Today we know that it is unfortunate that Heidegger connected the beginning of Greek philosophy with the revival of "the German university" in his Rectoral Address (1933). But my question is not about Heidegger's connection to National Socialism, but with his connection to the two great pre-Platonic thinkers, Heraclitus and Parmenides. One could say that the main topic for both thinkers was the same – Being. One was thinking about Being as a happening, and the second was thinking about Being as permanence. Would you agree with this?*

In my view, Heidegger's readings of Parmenides and Heraclitus (and of the Greeks generally) have no essential connection to his politics, and the matter of his politics is a separate topic for discussion, as you point out. Yet to your question about his readings of Parmenides and Heraclitus: Heidegger commented on both of these early Greek thinkers throughout his lifetime. Both thinkers remained important to him to the very end in his elucidation of the matter of Being.

In the traditional readings that you refer to, Parmenides is the thinker of "permanence" and Heraclitus is the thinker of "change" and "flux." Yet what is so engaging about Heidegger's account is that he considers these traditional readings to be fundamentally wrong or short-sighted; that is, he reads both Parmenides and Heraclitus as bringing to language Being as the *one* temporal "process" or "way" that includes or encompasses *both* "movement" and "rest as abiding." In other words, he understands these two early Greek thinkers as saying "the Same" (*das Selbe*) about Being but in different ways, and whether this is a "fair" or "accurate" reading remains open for debate. In any case, the larger point is this: One cannot fully understand Heidegger's original and distinctive understanding of Being/Beyng without appreciating his elucidations of Parmenides and Heraclitus. And this is why in *Heidegger's Way of Being*, I place so much emphasis in Chapters 5 and 6 on Heidegger's brilliant lecture courses on Heraclitus in 1943 and 1944, which have not received sufficient consideration in the scholarship.

The relation between Heidegger and Husserl remains a topic of discussion. How do you understand Heidegger's work in relation to Husserl's?

The relation between the thinking of Husserl and Heidegger is quite complex and would require a much longer answer, but I would offer this overview. Already in 1919, Heidegger began to take issue with Husserl's phenomenological perspective, yet in some other ways, he remained within Husserl's transcendental-phenomenological framework throughout the 1920s, including in *Being and Time*. Heidegger's break from transcendental-phenomenology is much more decisive in the 1930s and in later years. He came to understand Husserl's "phenomenology" as another version of the modern "subjectivism" or "subjectism" that was inaugurated by Descartes. In other words, Husserl never did arrive at "the things themselves" because his thinking was so strongly inflected toward transcendental subjectivity (*noesis*) and its "constitution" of the objects (*noema*) of thought. Now, whether Husserl's transcendental idealism is, in the end, a metaphysical idealism remains very much in question – even among Husserl scholars. Nevertheless, the point is that Heidegger came to see Husserl as largely trapped within a modern tradition of thinking that was so focused on human subjectivity that it had "forgotten" *Being*. It is in this context that Heidegger made a concerted effort to retrieve Aristotle's more originary thinking (and ancient Greek thinking generally) in order to overcome the prevailing "subjectism" of the modern age. Heidegger thought it was necessary to get back behind the modern thinking from Descartes to Kant to Husserl and return to the "origins" of Western thinking among the Greeks in order to recover the richest thinking – and experience – of Being.

In Heidegger's researches on Parmenides and Heraclitus over many years, he emphasized a new understanding of "aletheia" as "unconcealedness." In what do you see the sameness or difference in their understanding of truth?

As I noted in an earlier response, whatever the traditional thinking may be about the difference between Parmenides and Heraclitus, for Heidegger these two thinkers say "the Same" (but not "the identical") about Being. Let us recall that Heidegger thought that *aletheia* and *physis* were both ancient Greek names for Being; thus, Being and *aletheia* and *physis* say the Same. In Heidegger's reading, Parmenides's *aletheia* names the *one* temporal unconcealment (manifestation, showing-forth) of all beings in which inheres a dimension of concealment (withdrawal, reserve). Likewise, Heraclitus's *physis* names the unitary arising or emergence of all beings in which inheres a dimension of concealment, and this is said especially by Heraclitus's fragment 123: *physis kryptesthai philei*. Consequently, for Heidegger, both Parmenides and Heraclitus speak the Same about Being as "the primordial truth" that shines forth but also holds back in reserve. Put another way, Being "is" *Aletheia* "is" *Physis*.

Your book Heidegger's Way of Being *is very rich, and you show the indisputable place of Heraclitus's thinking in Heidegger's philosophical thought of the question of Being. What do you think is an important point in Heraclitus's thought that was an impulse for Heidegger's own question of Being (Seinsfrage)?*

You are right to observe that my book *Heidegger's Way of Being* highlights Heidegger's readings of Heraclitus in the 1943 and 1944 lecture courses. These lecture courses are remarkable, and English-speaking readers and scholars have largely overlooked their importance because the German volume, GA 55, has not yet been translated into English [as of 2017]. In Chapters 5 and 6, I present translations and discussions of these texts that have not appeared before in the English-language scholarship, and I have highlighted the importance of Heraclitus's fragments for Heidegger's thinking.

I cannot identify just one "impulse" from Heraclitus because there are many. Broadly speaking, Heidegger elucidated his understanding of Being in terms of Heraclitus's key fragments on *physis* and on *Logos* (or what Heidegger calls "the primordial Logos," *der ursprüngliche Logos*). For Heidegger, Heraclitus's *physis* and *Logos* are among the earliest names for Being itself, and he unfolds this theme in a variety of striking ways. I hope that your readers will consult these chapters in the book along with a reading of GA 55 in order to appreciate the creativity of Heidegger's readings. To give just one example, consider the poetic philosophical way that Heidegger describes the relation of the human being (and all beings) to Being in terms of the theme and imagery of "breathing in and breathing out," which I discuss in Chapter 6.

It is well-known that Heidegger never answered two questions in interviews: the question about God and the question about what he was working on. I would like to ask you about Heidegger's understanding of God, and especially about his notion of "the last god" from his Contributions. *What did he mean by this?*

This is very difficult to say, especially with respect to his enigmatic references to "the last god" in *Beiträge*, as you mention. So, allow me to answer this question about "the gods" more generally. The matter of the significance of the gods in Heidegger's thinking is difficult, but we should at least keep in view that he always insisted that "the gods" are never mere projections of the human being; that is, "the gods," no less than we "mortals," emerge from out of Being, the temporal-spatial emerging or unfolding "way" (or ontological process) wherein and whereby all beings issue forth and come to be. Certainly, for Heidegger, the "gods" or "divinities" are not traditional onto-theological timeless entities, for they, too, are "temporal" as they emerge from out of the temporal way itself – Being – their "Source," as he says.

Some recent readings of Heidegger – which are no more than variations of Husserl's transcendental idealism – are off the mark to suggest that, for the later Heidegger, the human being is the "source" of "Being," and, accordingly, these readings are also mistaken in trying to settle the matter of "the gods" in his thinking by claiming them for the human being, that is, by claiming that "the gods" are only insofar as the human being is. Heidegger – at every turn – upends this kind of position. His point is always that we have to learn once more how to be attentive and *listen*. Ours is the age of "egoity" (*Ichheit*) and of the increasing demand to make the human being the measure of all things. Heidegger calls on us to remain "open" to "the gods," but I must admit that it remains uncertain what Heidegger precisely means by these "gods" or "divinities." I suspect that he deliberately kept the matter uncertain in the service of questioning and thinking.

Nevertheless, as I have more recently discussed in my courses, the later Heidegger also spoke of "the divine God" (*das göttliche Gott*) or "the Godhead of God" (*die Gottheit des Gottes*), and he invited us to think of the divine as beyond what he had called the "the gods" of the Fourfold. In other words, he hinted that the "Godhead of God" is the ultimate mystery that is somehow at the heart of Being itself.

And, finally, I would like to ask you to suggest productive ways for future research into Heidegger's work.

As you know, at the present time there is a great deal of discussion about Heidegger's personal life and politics, but I think that we must keep in mind that no matter how strenuous the effort made by some recently, the distinction between Heidegger the man in his times and Heidegger the thinker cannot be collapsed. The creative work of any person can never be reduced to biography. If we keep this in mind, then there will continue to be ample room for us to admire and appreciate the depth of his thinking and for us to learn several essential philosophical and existential lessons from his work. I encourage young scholars to engage Heidegger's thinking with an open mind and an open heart.

To conclude, I wish to thank you, Vladimír, and your colleagues and readers for this opportunity to share my thoughts. I look forward to future exchanges with your philosophical community.

PART II

Translation

1 Martin Heidegger's Thinking and Japanese Philosophy

KŌICHI TSUJIMURA

Reply in Appreciation

MARTIN HEIDEGGER

TRANSLATED BY RICHARD CAPOBIANCO
AND MARIE GÖBEL

An Address in Celebration, September 26, 1969[1]

Most honored Professor Heidegger!
Most honored Mrs. Heidegger!
Honorable Mayor Schühle!
Ladies and Gentlemen!

It is a great honor not only for me alone but also for Japanese philosophy that I may deliver an address here today at the celebration of the 80th birthday of our great thinker. For this opportunity, I very sincerely thank those who have organized this celebration.

The reason that this honorable task has been given to me, an unknown Japanese, is presumably that I, a Japanese student of Heidegger, am coming from *afar*, if I may say so. Yet in the background of this coming from afar lies quite a long path, along which up until now many Japanese have tried, indeed are trying more and more today, to come into the nearness of the place where the thinking of our master sojourns. For this reason, please allow me to recall briefly some important predecessors along this path.

It was in 1921 when for the first time a Japanese studied with our thinker, who was lecturing in Freiburg at the time. His name is T. Yamanouchi, who later founded the seminar on Greek philosophy at the University of Kyōto. One year later in 1922, my teacher H. Tanabe came to Freiburg. He was, as far as I can tell, the first to discover the importance of Heideggerian thinking – not only in Japan, but perhaps in the entire world as well. In his essay from 1924 *The New Turn in Phenomenology – Heidegger's Phenomenology of Life*, one can already recognize a first version of *Being and Time*. Tanabe continued his thoughtful dialogue with Heidegger's thinking up until his death in 1962 and has remained the leading thinker in Japan. He once said to me in his last years: "In my opinion, Heidegger is the *only* thinker since Hegel." Then Baron Sh. Kuki came to see Heidegger in Marburg. To him we Japanese owe the first reliable elucidation of *Being and Time*. Unfortunately, he died too early – in 1941. In the troubled time of the thirties, my teacher and my predecessor as the Chair at the University of Kyōto, K. Nishitani, attended Heidegger's lectures on Nietzsche in Freiburg. Through Nishitani's profound interpretation, Heidegger's later reflections, as for example in his essay on *The Origin of the Work of Art*, became accessible to us. As far as I can see, he is today among those who understand Heidegger's thinking most deeply. Thus, in Japan, and particularly at the University of Kyōto, there has been an appropriation and tradition of Heideggerian thinking that has continued for almost half a century already. And so, also on behalf of my teachers and predecessors whom I have just mentioned, I must here express our heartfelt admiration and gratitude to Professor Heidegger.

The rather long path that I have indicated shows that, for us, Heidegger's thinking stands in a particularly important relation to Japanese philosophy. Hence, the title of the address, which for our part would like to be an address of thanks: "Martin Heidegger's Thinking and Japanese Philosophy."

In order to shed some light on this relationship, we must first proceed from a determination of the essence – and the distress of that essence [*Wesensnot*] – of Japanese philosophy. If one understands Japanese philosophy in the sense of philosophy *in* Japan, then in Japan there are also almost all of the movements of contemporary philosophy. Nearly all of them have been introduced to us from Europe and America, and, consequently, are not for us a home-grown thinking. If, however, we understand by Japanese philosophy that thinking endeavor which does not arise from the place of Western European philosophy, but rather springs from the ground source [*Quellgrund*] of our own spiritual tradition, then this philosophy is something very rare. In what follows, I understand Japanese philosophy in the latter sense – and this philosophy finds itself in an essential distress.

From the most ancient times, we Japanese have been close to nature in a specific sense. Namely: We do not have the will to dominate nature, but instead we want to live and die as far as possible in a way that is in accord with nature. On his deathbed, a simple Japanese said to those around him: "I am dying now, just as leaves fall in the autumn." And a Zen Buddhist master, who was, so to speak, the grandfather of my own Zen practice, refused an injection when he was dying and said: "What is the point of such a forcing and, thereby, of a prolonged life?" Instead of taking the medicine, he took a sip of his favorite rice wine and died calmly. Rightly understood, here already is evident a stark contrast between the age-old Japanese spiritual tradition and a life determined by the European spiritual tradition and by European science and technology. In short, to live and die in accord with nature was, we may say, an ideal of the ancient Japanese wisdom of life.

Now, of course, this does not mean that we Japanese have no will, but it says that at the ground of the will nature prevails. The will is in the first and last instance born out of nature and will vanish into nature, this nature which assuredly withdraws from every scientific objectification and yet remains everywhere present. Nature, in Japanese "*shizen*" or "*zinen*," means: being as something is from itself forth – in brief: being-itself and being-true. For this reason, "nature" in the olden Japanese language was almost synonymous with "freedom" and "truth." This view of nature has been deepened by the Buddhist "insight into the transience and emptiness" of all things.

In order to bring to light the distress of the essence of Japanese philosophy in the sense just given, let us briefly turn our attention to the other side of the matter. Ever since the Europeanization of Japan that began some 100 years ago, we have with all our might introduced European culture and civilization into almost all spheres of our life. The Europeanization has been an historical necessity for us so that we Japanese can maintain our independence in the modern world, that is to say, in the sphere of power that is determined by the will. Yet, at the same time, therein lies the danger that we can lose our ownmost essence which has been indicated. In order to avoid this consequence in the past, the Europeanization of Japan happened on the whole without an inner connection to our own spiritual tradition. Since then we have had to suffer a deep conflict at the core of our Dasein, namely, the conflict between our own way of living and thinking in accord with nature and the strongly will-determined Western way of living and thinking that has been imposed on us from outside. This conflict first of all remains veiled in an optimistic way, and yet visible all the same, in a slogan that appeared back then, namely: "Japanese spirit with European ability." What is meant by this ability is above all modern science and technology. The conflict still exists today in our everyday life. We "Europeanized Japanese" must more or less lead a double life.

To bring this conflict in some way into a primordial unity should be, in my opinion, the authentic task of a Japanese philosophy. However, apart from a few attempts, it has not yet succeeded in accomplishing this. Instead, Japanese philosophy has itself remained for the most part in the same unmediated conflictedness of the "Japanese spirit with European ability" and, indeed, to an even greater degree. The many and diverse movements of European philosophy that we have tried to transplant in our country since the second half of the past century could not take root in our ground. Rather, nearly all of them remained merely imitated by us like a fashion or at most employed in a limited area of our societal life such as in science and technology. Consequently, the term "Japanese philosophy" is already a marker for the fundamental distress of its essence. This distress issues, on the one hand, from the fact that we adopted European philosophy without an essential engagement of the aforementioned ground source of our own spiritual tradition, and, on the other hand, from the fact that most of the philosophical movements were not able to touch us and shake us right down to this very ground source of our spiritual life.

Yet with Heidegger's thinking the matter stands altogether differently. What becomes worthy of questioning through his thinking is what we always already are and so what is already somehow understood by us in a non-objective way, and thus is always overlooked in science and philosophy. It seems to me that the matter [Sache] of Heidegger's thinking always preserves this character. For this reason, the matter of his thinking withdraws itself in its truth as soon as we simply want to represent, grasp, and know it. And, therefore, his thinking remains in principle inimitable. The ultimate matter of his thinking, which perhaps may be indicated by the ancient Greek word *Alētheia* (un-concealedness), could be understood in view of Western philosophy, and that means here metaphysics, as a ground that is concealed to metaphysics itself. Thus, the matter itself would have demanded from the thinker a transformation of thinking – namely, the transformation of philosophical thinking into "another thinking." Only by this other thinking – and that means by "the step back from philosophy" – has what is "proper" to philosophical thinking – and that means here what is proper to the essence of the Western world and of its humanity – been "properly" glimpsed. That is an extraordinary appropriating event [*Ereignis*]. In this sense, we Japanese see in Heidegger's thinking a glimpsing-of-itself of what is "proper" to Western humanity and its world.

In view of this thinking, we Japanese, too, necessarily had to be thrown back onto the forgotten ground of our own spiritual tradition. If I may offer something personal here: Right after my first encounter with *Being and Time* when I was still in secondary school, I sensed that at least for us Japanese the only possible access to a genuine understanding of this work of thinking is concealed in our tradition of Zen Buddhism. And this is so because Zen Buddhism is nothing other than a seeing-through

[*Durchblicken*] to what we ourselves are. For this seeing-through, we first have to let go of all representing, producing, adjusting, altering, acting, making, and willing, in short, all consciousness and its activity, and then, following along such a way, to return to its ground source. As one of the greatest Zen masters, Dōgen, says as well: "You shall first learn the step back." (Dōgen, *Fukanzazengi*).[2]

Nevertheless, what does Heidegger's thinking have to do with East-Asian Zen Buddhism at all? From the perspective of this thinking, perhaps nothing since it is an altogether independent thinking. Yet from our perspective, we have a great deal to do with that thinking. For now, we must limit ourselves to mentioning only a few things concerning the peculiar relation between Heidegger's thinking and our Zen Buddhism; this may be accomplished by turning to the example of the "blooming tree" that Heidegger speaks about one time (cf. *Was heißt Denken?* p. 16ff.).[3]

The tree there blooms. Regarding this simple situation Heidegger speaks as follows: "We stand before a blooming tree – and the tree stands before us." Anyone can say this. Heidegger restates this matter then in this way: "We place ourselves [*stellen uns*] face-to-face with a tree, before it, and the tree presents itself to us [*stellt sich uns vor*]." Here already appears the peculiarity of his thinking. As I understand it, one usually says in German: We present to ourselves (dative) a tree. Instead of this Heidegger says: "We place ourselves (accusative) face-to-face with a tree, before it." What happens in this restating? Perhaps nothing other than the disappearing of the "we" as representing subject and, simultaneously, of the "tree" as represented object.

Since Descartes, thinking always means *I* think, that is, *I* present *to myself*. This fact, that I *think*, Descartes understands from the: *I* think. *Cogito* means: cogito *me* cogitare. From this comes henceforth the philosophy of transcendental Idealism, and it informs the Schopenhauerian principle: the world is my representation. To the contrary, Heidegger restates the matter in the way just mentioned. The matter, that we stand before a blooming tree and the tree stands before us, our thinker thinks or sees no longer from the "*I* think," but from the "there" where the tree stands, which is the ground "upon which we live and die." In this restatement, we have "leapt out of the familiar territory of the sciences and even ... of philosophy." In view of the simple situation that the tree there blooms, we, as representing subject, and the tree, as represented object, must vanish into another kind of "representing." Otherwise, we would not be able at all to see in truth the tree there blooming. Zen Buddhism characterizes this matter in this way, for example: "The donkey looks into the well and the well looks into the donkey. The bird looks at the flower and the flower looks at the bird."

This other "re-presenting," wherein the tree presents itself and the human being places himself face-to-face with the tree, we could perhaps call a *released* representing, whereas that "I present to myself" can be called, as it were, a *willful* representing. From this to that we must leap. Concerning this leap, Heidegger speaks as follows: We must first "leap onto the ground upon which we live and die," that is, "upon which we truly stand." Only by this peculiar leap is a field opened in which "the tree and we are." In this field, called "region" [*Gegnet*], the tree presents itself to us as what it is, and we place ourselves, such as we are, face-to-face with the blooming tree. Yet this field is wherein already from the beginning we dwell and the tree stands there blooming.

I would like to cite now a somewhat corresponding example from Zen Buddhism. It is a very famous kōan that is a Zen-question. Once a monk asked master Chao-chou: "For what reason did the first patriarch Boddhidharma come to China?" To this Chao-chou answers: "cypress tree in the garden." The monk inquired further: "Master – please do not indicate with the help of an object!" Chao-chou said: "I am not indicating with the help of an object." Then the monk asked anew: "For what reason did the first patriarch Boddhidharma come to China?" Chao-chou answered: "cypress tree in the garden."

It is perfectly clear that the first patriarch came from India to China to convey the Buddhist truth. Therefore, the monk's question means: "What is the first and last truth of Zen Buddhism?" Chao-chou's reply is quite simply: "cypress tree in the garden." This answer illuminates like a bolt of lightning, which, with one

blow, knocked to the ground the question along with the questioning monk and, at the same time, allows to flash up, completely unveiled, the truth that was sought. With such a manner
of responding, the monk should have suddenly leapt onto the
ground upon which he and the cypress tree already are. But the
lightning did not penetrate the questioning monk. He did not
pay attention to Chao-chou's answers themselves, but rather to
what was said, that is, the "cypress tree in the garden" as represented object. Consequently, he had to request: "Do not indicate
(the truth) with the help of an object." Since from the beginning
Master Chao-chou has not shown the truth with the help of an
object, his answer to the question posed again is precisely as
before. But the monk does not make the leap; that is, he does not
attain awakening. He remains chained to objectifying representing, seeing, and thinking.

If I may add something further, Mr. Chao-chou did not have to
give precisely this answer: "cypress tree in the garden." Where
the tree is, as what it is, and where we are, such as we are, there
unfolds [west] everywhere Buddhist truth, which, exactly for this
reason, no longer needs to be designated specifically as *Buddhist*
truth. The first patriarch did not have to come over the danger-
ous sea to China at all. *Nevertheless*, he had to come. Nevertheless, Mr. Chao-chou had to say expressly: "cypress tree in the
garden." Nevertheless, Mr. Heidegger must think, question, and
say expressly, for example: "We must first leap onto the ground
upon which we live and die." Why is this "nevertheless" necessary? Because we must first leap onto the ground upon which
we live and die. Because in the forgottenness of the ground upon
which we tread, we always wander astray to and fro. Even Chao-
chou's answer "cypress in the garden" can mislead us. We must
make such an answer superfluous.

In short, between the "peculiar leap" that is spoken of by
Heidegger and our "we do not need to at all – and nevertheless...," there is a deeply concealed relation, as it appears to me.
Heidegger asks: "What comes to pass [*ereignet sich*] here that
the tree presents itself to us and we place ourselves face-to-face
with the tree?" With him, we could perhaps answer: "The region
gathers together, just as if nothing were coming to pass, each

to each and everything to one another into the abiding, while reposing in itself" (*Gelassenheit*, p. 41ff.).[4] This "region," stated from our perspective, is the "field of the Buddha," that is, the field of truth. Assuming that the Japanese Zen master Dōgen had heard Heidegger's question, he would have perhaps answered: "In the very moment when an old plum tree comes into bloom, in its blooming the world comes to pass" (Dōgen, *Shōbōgenzō*, Ch. *Baika*).[5]

At the end of his example of the blooming tree, Heidegger had warned and challenged: "What matters before all else, and finally, is not to let fall away the blooming tree, but for once to let it stand there where it stands" (*Was heißt Denken?* p. 18).[6] We are also warned in Zen, although in another context but with fundamentally one and the same meaning, by that kōan "cypress tree in the garden": "Do not fell, do not bring down that sprawling tree, since in its cool shade human beings repose."

Taking into account what has been said, we can now perhaps summarize in the following manner: Heidegger's thinking and Zen Buddhism are, at the very least, in accord in knocking representational thinking to the ground. The field of truth that is thereby opened shows that in both there is a very intimate relation that has not yet been sufficiently clarified. However, while Zen Buddhism has not yet arrived at clarifying *in a thinking way* the field of truth, or more precisely, of un-truth with respect to its essential features, Heidegger's thinking unceasingly attempts to bring to light the essential features of *Alētheia* (un-concealment). This difference makes us aware of a shortcoming in Zen Buddhism – at least in its heretofore traditional form. What traditional Zen Buddhism is lacking is an epochal thinking and questioning of the world. Regarding this question of the world, we must learn and appropriate something decisive from Heidegger's thinking – in particular from his extraordinary notion of the "enframing" as the essence of technology. Otherwise, Zen Buddhism itself would have to become a barren tree. Otherwise, no path could be cleared from Zen to a possible Japanese philosophy.

This evening is a celebration. Our elder, great thinker has come home. In order to celebrate his homecoming, I would like to conclude this address of celebration and of thanks with an old poem or ours:

"Let us return home! Toward the south, north, east, and west. In the deep of the night, we see together the snow on thousand-layered cliffs."

From Martin Heidegger's Reply in Appreciation[7]

These days I often think back, and particularly now, on the celebration of my seventieth birthday that was so delightfully happy. To me, it seems as if it were today; and, yet, a decade lies in-between. In this short space of time, the restless world has been shaped by rapidly successive changes. The past expectation, admittedly already in doubt, that the homeliness of the homeland [*das Heimatliche der Heimat*] could still be immediately saved – this expectation we may no longer cherish. The expression that I wrote in 1946 to a French friend speaks more precisely to this point: "Homelessness is the fate of the world" [*Über den Humanismus*, Frankfurt a.M., first edition, 1949, p. 27].[8] Modern man is settling himself into this homelessness.

Yet this homelessness conceals itself behind a phenomenon that my friend Tsujimura has already indicated and that I call for short "the world civilization," which a century ago broke in upon Japan as well. World civilization, that means today: the dominance of the natural sciences, the dominance and primacy of the economy, politics, technology. Everything else is no longer even a superstructure [*Überbau*], but merely an utterly run-down annex [*Nebenbau*].[9]

We find ourselves in this world civilization. The engagement of thinking is dedicated to this. In the meantime, this world civilization has reached across the whole earth. Therefore, Mr. Tsujimura, our distress is the same as yours. You have demanded quite a bit from the people of Messkirch and from myself with your attempt to make Zen Buddhism "understandable" through a few examples. I cannot say more about that here; however, I would like to mention a fact that is perhaps also familiar to you.

In 1929, as the successor of my teacher Husserl at Freiburg, I delivered my inaugural lecture with the title "What is Metaphysics?" In this lecture, the "nothing" was discussed; I made the attempt to point out that "Being," in contrast to all "beings," is no "being" and, in this sense, is a "nothing." German philosophy, as well as philosophy abroad, characterized this address as "nihilism." In the following year, 1930, a young Japanese man by the name of Yuassa, who was as old as your son perhaps and of the same build, translated into Japanese this lecture that he heard – he was in his first semester. He understood what this lecture wanted to show. This shall suffice as a reply to your address. I thank you and ask you to greet the Japanese friends and, above all, your trusted teacher, Professor Nishitani, whose successor you are; and with me to treasure the memory of his teacher, Professor Tanabe, who in 1922, when I myself was still a beginner, came to Freiburg where I tried to familiarize him with the basic features and methods of "phenomenological thinking." He became Japan's most significant thinker and died a solitary man in the mountains, probably in the manner as you have just sketched it.

PART III

Reflections and Impressions

1 Heidegger and the Earliest Greeks

Heidegger and the Greeks. Heidegger scholars and readers must always keep this topic in view and in consideration. How do things stand between Heidegger's "core matter" (*die Sache selbst*) and the Greeks?

The extraordinary upshot of *Introduction to Metaphysics* (IM) is that Heidegger stated clearly and decisively that "truth belongs to the unfolding of Being." As I highlighted this in *Heidegger's Way of Being*, 58–62, his reflections on Being/*physis*/*aletheia* after *Being and Time* are brought to a culminating point in IM in 1935: Being "is" *physis* "is" *aletheia* as emergence/showing forth/shining forth. The remarkable boldness and originality of Heidegger's position must not be overlooked. In his view, the whole history of Western philosophical thinking, beginning with Plato, progressively determined the primary locus of "truth" to be the human being (or the divine being in medieval philosophy and theology). Heidegger upends this subjectist trajectory in the history of Western philosophy and states that, in the first place, *Being is truth as emergence*. Being "is" *aletheia*.

Some have inquired about the relation of Heidegger's reading of Being/*physis*/*aletheia* to his comments at the end of IM that appear to move away from the Greeks. Yet there is no difficulty, and here is why: In the last part of IM, Heidegger critiqued the understanding of Being as it devolved into *physis* as *ousia* as "constant presence" in Plato and Aristotle (*eidos, idea, morphe*, and later *essentia*, essence). Yet this said, we should also keep in mind that Heidegger always found echoes of the earlier Greek understanding of Being in Plato and Aristotle, and for that reason, his criticism of Plato and Aristotle was always careful and nuanced. Still, Heidegger did detect the devolution of thinking in these two great "philosophers."

Thus as I see it, Heidegger regarded the *earliest* Greek thinkers Anaximander, Parmenides, and Heraclitus (but also Homer, Pindar, and Sophocles) to have brought to light – however glancingly – the core matter for thought, that is, *das Zu-denkende*, the to-be-thought: Being itself as *Ereignis* as *Lichtung* as *Es gibt*. It is crucial to keep in mind that Heidegger never stated that the *earliest* Greek thinkers did not arrive at the core matter. He never tried to "get behind" the earliest Greek thinkers to recover or uncover a more primordial position, as he did with all subsequent thinkers in the tradition. Rather, he always sought to highlight that the earliest Greek thinkers did indeed have the fundamental matter in view. If there is a difference between the "first inception" and "the other inception," it is simply that in the latter, the core matter is thought explicitly and thematically. Otherwise, to think the first is to think the other, and to think the other is to think the first. Indeed, Heidegger says precisely this in the famous 1962 lecture "Time and Being": "Yet the sole aim of this lecture has been to bring into view Being itself as *Ereignis*," and this thinking of *Ereignis* as *Es gibt* is not new at all, but rather "the oldest of the old in Western thought: the most ancient that conceals itself in the name *A-letheia*" (GA 14: 26, 29).

Also, for Heidegger, the earliest Greek thinkers and poets had the same essential insight into Being *as* time. There are many texts to consider, but a little-known one is his commentary in 1932 on Sophocles' *Ajax* (GA 35, see also *Heidegger's Way of Being*, 55), where he maintains that Sophocles brought to light how "mighty, immeasurable time allows everything both to appear and disappear." Being as unfolding, Being-as-time, was not "concealed" to the *earliest* Greeks. Yet I would agree with those who would say that, according to Heidegger, this was then largely lost from view with the Greek "philosophers" and their successors, who understood the *ontos on*, the "really real," as unchangeable and "timeless."

After IM, when Heidegger delivered his remarkable lecture courses on Parmenides and Heraclitus in the early 1940s, he returned to Being as *physis* as *aletheia* and also as the primordial *Logos*. In the 1944 Heraclitus lecture course, Heidegger stated the following, which indicates most clearly that throughout his lifetime of thinking when he spoke about the earliest Greek understanding of *physis* and *aletheia* and the primordial *Logos* (among several other Greek *Ur*-words), he was always also speaking about his ownmost concern with – and his ownmost experience of – the fundamental matter of Being itself. Thus he stated that to think along with Heraclitus, it is clear:

> that nothing higher, nothing more primordial, nothing more present, but also nothing more inapparent and nothing more indestructible can be thought than Beyng itself.
>
> (GA 55: 278; also *Heidegger's Way of Being*, 84–6)

2 Heidegger, Phenomenology, and Metaphysics

There remains confusion around the matter of Heidegger, phenomenology, and metaphysics, and it is useful to offer a few indications to help clarify things.

First, when many commentators today oppose Heidegger's "phenomenological" approach to any "metaphysical" approach, what they principally have in mind is that Heidegger's approach demands of us that we take into account our "experience" of what we bring to language. It is this experiential or existential dimension that is contrasted with the alleged neutrality or impersonality of traditional metaphysical thought that deals only with detached "assumptions" and "propositions."

There is truth to this if we are speaking about "textbook" approaches to metaphysics, but it is certainly a dubious assertion if we consider the thought of many of the great metaphysicians, from Plato to Whitehead. In their work, metaphysical statements about the nature and structure of things are rooted in an existential context. Metaphysical statements are appropriated as experiential – and this would seem to be precisely what Heidegger was getting at in speaking of his aim to "ground" metaphysics. That is, our task is to dig deep to find the "living root" of metaphysical statements and positions.

Consequently, if by "phenomenology" we mean taking into consideration the experiential dimension of our words and positions, then there is no *necessary* opposition to metaphysics at all. However, if some further insist on the strict understanding of phenomenology as an investigation into the meaning-making structure of the human being that prohibits making statements about how things are in themselves, then, indeed, there opens up an opposition. In this case, phenomenology takes on the form of an idealism/subjectivism/constructivism that is opposed to a metaphysical realism. Yet this strict or narrow understanding of phenomenology is hardly ever intended these days by those who use the word; the term has migrated into the vernacular and into the general academic vocabulary to signify little more than a focus on how we human beings "experience" anything whatsoever. Accordingly, it is no wonder that strict phenomenologists in the classical Husserlian sense worry that phenomenology is fading into oblivion – or that it has been supplanted by an Analytic "philosophy of mind."

Yet there is a second issue of concern. There are two different narratives in Heidegger's work regarding metaphysics. One narrative he put into play was that he was not opposed to metaphysics but rather wished only to "ground" metaphysical statements in our lived experience. This is the Heidegger we have just mentioned whose hermeneutic phenomenology does not propose to "destroy" or "overcome" metaphysics but rather to appropriate it. One of his important later statements in this vein is his 1949 "Introduction to 'What is Metaphysics?'" (GA 9).

Nevertheless, there is another narrative. In some places, he spoke harshly about metaphysics and claimed that it must be "overcome." This is the Heidegger who unfortunately set into motion the ritual denunciation of all metaphysical thinking that we encounter in so much postmodern and contemporary Continental thinking. Yet more careful and nuanced reflection is required. What *kind* of metaphysical thinking did Heidegger wish to "overcome"? I think it is clear that his target was chiefly any version of *a substance or subject metaphysics*. His earliest and enduring insight was into Being-as-time, and thus he bristled at any traditional metaphysical view that identified *timeless* substances or essences with Being itself. This is the Heidegger who was indeed determined to overcome any such kind of metaphysical position, which he derogatorily characterized as "ontotheological" thinking.

There are no doubt important insights and merits to Heidegger's critique, but one flaw in his narrative was that he overstated the case. He set himself the task of showing how every epoch of philosophical thinking subsequent to the "earliest Greek thinkers" (Anaximander, Parmenides, Heraclitus) constructed "onto-theological" positions. Yet there are difficulties with this claim. To cite just one example, is not the Neoplatonic "One" *beyond* (*epekeina*) all categories such as substance and essence? Is it not the case, then, that Heidegger sometimes oversimplified past metaphysical positions in order to ultimately dismiss them as "onto-theological"? We must further interrogate his thinking on this matter.

Nevertheless, by clarifying that Heidegger's opposition to metaphysics was chiefly an opposition to a substance metaphysics ("onto-theology"), then we see that Heidegger's thinking of Being is not necessarily opposed to metaphysics *as such*. It remains for us to consider whether alternative forms of metaphysics – a dynamic "process" metaphysics, for example – are compatible with Heidegger's thinking of Being-as-time-as-unfolding process. Metaphysics need not be a substance metaphysics. If we keep this in mind, then we realize that it is possible to consider that some versions of metaphysical thinking may be compatible with Heidegger's thinking of Being-as-time. Metaphysics transformed, maybe, but not "overcome."

3 Why "Phenomenology" Inevitably Slides toward Idealism/ Subjectivism/Constructivism

To put this in a nutshell: Husserl's "phenomenology" and all related versions (including the early Heidegger's hermeneutic phenomenology) speak about returning to "the things themselves," but transcendental-phenomenology (hereafter, t-p) never *attains* to the things themselves. Rather, t-p returns again and again to the intellective or noetic (or "existential") conditions of the possibility of knowing something, and thus remains fixated on "knowing our knowing." T-p is really not more than a continuation of the modern project of epistemology or philosophy of mind. Or to put this another way, t-p is much like Zeno's Achilles who must always traverse half the distance to get to the other side of the field and thus never arrives on the other side. T-p never arrives at "the things themselves"; it remains at the starting line of asking *how* knowing x or y is possible in the first place.

Nevertheless, certain advocates of t-p (most often the so-called "East Coast Husserlians") argue that t-p is compatible with a metaphysical realism, but this is dubious. T-p proceeds with an analysis of the conditions of our knowing something, or what some call the "normative conditions and orders" of our knowing something. Yet this means that t-p is always inflected toward human subjectivity in such a way that being or "the real" is, in the end, construed as "measured out" by these noetic or normative conditions. The focus is on the clarification of the noetic/normative conditions, which puts at a distance "the things themselves" in favor of a clarification of how things are "constituted" by us and thereby appear to us.

When proponents of t-p argue that normative orders "only measure what they measure," they reinforce the fundamental Cartesian idea that it is the noetic analysis that is "certain" and reliable (and therefore the proper work of philosophy); whereas the content of the noema ("the thing itself") is, in contrast, always incomplete and dubious and not the proper concern for philosophy. In the end, t-p is an epistemological enterprise that is always inclined toward an idealism or subjectivism that seeks to deliver clear and distinct knowledge about the noetic normative conditions of consciousness (or about Dasein's "projective" activity).

Many who consider themselves "phenomenologists" are perfectly content with this conclusion because they have renounced any kind of metaphysical realism. Yet there are other distinguished t-p thinkers who are thoughtful enough not to accept this facile conclusion. They have tried to maintain that t-p, even as Husserl understood it, is compatible with a metaphysical realism. They have tried, but they have not been convincing.

In a metaphysical realist view, things are and have a certain structure independent of our noetic access. Yet the most that t-p can conclude is a *metaphysical neutrality*; that is, the "things themselves" remain forever under question or "bracketed." T-p cannot say anything about how things are independent of our noetic access to them, and thus, again, t-p falls back on an analysis of the structures of human subjectivity that permit or condition anything at all to appear to us *as* this or that. Thus t-p is necessarily limited to a metaphysical neutrality. Yet, consequently, t-p is always one short step away from a purely idealist, subjectivist, or constructivist view of "world" or "reality" that installs the human being as the measure of all things. Some defenders of t-p rightly recoil from this development and argue against it, but they, too, must understand why, strictly speaking, "phenomenology" – whether Husserl's or even the early Heidegger's – always slides inevitably toward idealism or subjectivism or constructivism. And after *Being and Time*, Heidegger recognized this as well.

4   Heidegger's "Clearing" Is Not Identical with the Human Being

This is an issue that I have discussed in detail in both *Engaging Heidegger* and *Heidegger's Way of Being*; nevertheless, it is a matter that is still overlooked or confused by some Heidegger commentators and therefore requires reiteration and added emphasis. In one respect, the matter was already decisively settled by Heidegger in *Letter on Humanism* (1947) when he raised the issue of "*die Lichtung*" or "the clearing" and emphatically stated: "But the clearing itself is Being" ("*Die Lichtung selber ist das Sein*," GA 9: 332), and *not* the human being.

Yet Heidegger gave us a fuller description of his revision of his early position on *die Lichtung* in an important talk from 1965 titled "On the Question Concerning the Determination of the Matter for Thinking."[1] Any study of Heidegger's understanding of the clearing must take into account his remarks in this talk, and, more specifically, his explicit revision of his earlier understanding of the clearing in *Being and Time*. He concedes in this talk that his earlier characterization of *die Lichtung* was inadequate and did not yet arrive at the core matter for thinking, namely, that the clearing *grants* human Dasein in the first place. Consequently, this text offers us further evidence of "the turn" in his later thinking, and it also brings into sharper focus his decisive statement in *Letter on Humanism* that "the clearing itself is Being." This text and the whole matter of "the clearing" I discussed at length in both *Engaging Heidegger* (Chapters 5 and 6) and *Heidegger's Way of Being* (Chapter 1).

At one point in this talk, he notes that he had made mention of the clearing in "his hermeneutic analytic of Dasein" in *Being and Time* and that this notion of the clearing had been taken up by Ludwig Binswanger in the development of his psychiatric "Daseinsanalysis." But Heidegger proceeds to clarify that the clearing is *not* identical with the human being, and he gives us a crucial insight into the development of his own thinking on this matter:

> Yet it required a decades-long walk along those forest paths that lead only so far to realize that the sentence in *Being and Time*: "The Dasein of the human being is itself the clearing" (§28), perhaps surmised the matter for thinking but in no way considered the matter adequately, that is, in no way posed the matter as a question that arrived at the matter.
>
> The Dasein is the clearing for presence as such, and yet Dasein is, at the same time, certainly not the clearing insofar as the clearing is Dasein in the first place, that is, insofar as the clearing grants Dasein as such [in the first place]. The analytic of Dasein does not yet attain to what is proper to the clearing and by no means attains to the region to which the clearing, in turn, belongs.
>
> (GA 16: 631)

This is the key passage. It is Heidegger's *retractatio* on the matter of *die Lichtung*. That is, what he said about the clearing in *Being and Time* was inadequate; it did not yet attain to the core matter. Only years later, he tells us, was he able to see and state that the clearing *grants* human Dasein in the first place. This is the core matter. And he adds, the clearing is "wherein we human beings always already sojourn. In this region, however, things linger in their own way" (632). In other words, it is not simply we humans who belong within the clearing; indeed, *all things belong within the clearing*.

Thus: the clearing, the region, Being itself – this is the fundamental matter for thought. We humans, along with all things, are granted by the clearing and sojourn within the clearing, which, as he stated in *Letter on Humanism*, "is Being."

Finally, to put an even finer point on this matter, let us consider Heidegger's firm and direct statement in his conversation with Medard Boss in 1963: "the human being is not the clearing itself, is not the whole clearing, is not identical with the whole clearing as such" (GA 89: 663).

5 Heidegger, Max Müller, and Metaphysics

"Heidegger Remains a Metaphysician"

Professor William J. Richardson (1920–2016) had a special relationship with Professor Max Müller (1906–1994), but what is also of particular interest is Müller's life-long relationship with Heidegger and Müller's own thoughts and observations on the major themes of Heidegger's thinking. Here is one important issue for consideration.

The Max Müller story is quite interesting in itself. The young Müller deeply admired Heidegger, and he was one of Heidegger's finest students in the late 1920s. Müller became involved in the Catholic Youth Movement (inspired by Romano Guardini among others) that opposed the National Socialists, and into the 1930s his relationship with Heidegger became strained. In 1937, Heidegger damaged Müller's chances of securing a lectureship, but after the conclusion of the Second World War – and this speaks to the complexity of life and of human relations – they reconciled; in fact, Müller was instrumental in Heidegger's "rehabilitation."

From the 1950s onward, Müller was one of Heidegger's closest and most trusted colleagues and friends until Heidegger's death in 1976. After the war, Müller spent several years at the University of Freiburg as Heidegger's colleague, and he became a successful teacher and scholar in his own right. Years later, in 1986, Müller published the fourth edition of his book *Existenzphilosophie* (ed. Alois Halder, Verlag Karl Alber, Freiburg). This edition is notable because in it he directly mentioned William Richardson's "great" book and offered his understanding of Heidegger's relation to "metaphysics." Müller's book and his comments have been overlooked in Anglophone Heidegger studies.

In the last section of this edition of the book, Müller observed that Heidegger could not accept the static "system" and "dogmatics" of the Neo-Scholastic metaphysical theology (356). Nevertheless, according to Müller, Heidegger was always concerned with the matter of "the history of God with the human being and of the human being with God." Furthermore, Müller stated, "Heidegger remains a metaphysician," with the proviso that we keep this dynamic and historical dimension of Being in view.

Müller proceeded to expand on this, and I offer a translation of his interesting comments that deserve further consideration (parentheses are Müller's, brackets are my insertions). For background: In the following passage, Müller is referring to Heidegger's request to Richardson, a request also frequently recounted by Richardson, that he change the title of his book from "Heidegger: *From* Phenomenology *to* Thought" to "Heidegger: *Through* Phenomenology to Thought." Richardson included the portrait photo and the poem (both mentioned in the passage) at the beginning of his book – but, as far as I can tell, Richardson never published anywhere that these two items were sent to him by Heidegger along with the Preface. Here is the passage from Müller:

Furthermore, for Martin Heidegger, metaphysics still belongs so very much to the humanness of the human being such that he says of metaphysics in "What is Metaphysics?": We cannot at all be transposed into metaphysics because we, insofar as we exist, always already stand in it. Thus Plato says (Phaedrus, 279a): φύσει γάρ, ὦ φίλε, ἔνεστί τις φιλοσοφία τῇ τοῦ ἀνδρὸς διανοίᾳ. ["For by nature, my friend, the human being's mind dwells in philosophy."] That is: Insofar as the human being is, philosophizing in a certain manner happens, namely, as metaphysics." This [statement] Martin Heidegger has never withdrawn.

In Heidegger's development and its self-understanding, two "passages" [Durchgänge] have played a decisive role: One, the passage through the classical, Aristotelian-oriented metaphysics; then there is the passage through the phenomenology inaugurated by

Edmund Husserl. Aristotle and Husserl were in equal measure
his teachers. The word "passage" was chosen by himself (Mar-
tin Heidegger). So when P. [Pater, Father] William J. Richardson
S.J., wrote his great Heidegger-book "Through Phenomenology to
Thought" ("*Durch die Phänomenologie zum Seins-Denken*"), to which
Heidegger provided not only the introductory Preface, but also
a photo of himself and perhaps his most lovely youthful poem
"*Abendgang auf der Reichenau*," Heidegger insisted that the original
[words] "From – to" in the title should be replaced with "*Durch*"
(Through). And this means that Heidegger in his self-understanding did not surrender either phenomenology or metaphysics; it is
one and the same path that led through them and that he never
abandoned, and is the way upon which he remained and maintained as his path. But he travels along this same path further. Yet
to where does this "further" lead?   (356–7)

Indeed, where does it lead? As Müller understood, one path
leads toward a revised understanding of metaphysics.

6 Heidegger, Plato, and "Light"

From start to finish, Heidegger was fascinated by the image and theme of "light," and it is central to all of his thinking of Being. As early as 1919, in one of his first uses of his signature term *Ereignis*, Heidegger cited poetic lines from Sophocles' *Antigone* to exemplify a vibrant, resonant "happening" in our lived experience: the splendor of the rising and shining sun. In retrospect, we see that this is a perfect prefiguring of his reading in subsequent years of *phainomenon* in terms of *phainesthai* in terms of *phos* – light (*lux*). Things "shining forth" – arising, emerging in resplendence (see also *Heidegger's Way of Being*, Chapter 1).

Heidegger was indebted to Plato's fundamental philosophical theme of "light," and he was also no doubt influenced by the medieval "metaphysics of light" as represented by Robert Grosseteste, for example (also *Engaging Heidegger*, Chapters 5 and 6). Despite Heidegger's attraction to this guiding theme of light to characterize his understanding of Being as the temporal radiant unfolding of all things, he was, nonetheless, also ambivalent.

He was concerned that Plato's "light" was too "metaphysical," namely, that it was centered on being as timeless and unchanging. This is why in his multiple readings of Plato's "Allegory of the Cave," he sought to rescue the Idea of the Good from a substance/essence metaphysics by arguing that the Good (= the sun) is the "light of lights," or, in other words, that it is the "light" that *enables* or makes possible in the first place any substance/essence metaphysics. Even so, in the middle and later years, it is evident that Heidegger had misgivings about the theme of "light." Plato's "light" shone too brightly (or Plato's "shadow" loomed too large), and Heidegger made an effort to put into play his own theme of a spatial "clearing" in order to distance his thinking of Being from the Platonic tradition of "light" (*lux*).

Yet, alas, to no avail, because Heidegger continued to employ the image and theme of "light" (*lux*) to the very end of his life. It remained central to his thinking and to his vision of Being. This is perhaps best illustrated in one of Heidegger's very late writings (1976), a beautiful little commentary on one of Hölderlin's so-called last poems. The title of the poem is "Autumn," and the opening line is "Nature's gleaming is higher revealing," which I discuss in detail in *Heidegger's Way of Being*, Chapter 2. Yet what I wish to underscore here is that Heidegger's commentary attests to his own profound sense of the *gleaming* unfolding of all things – a sense that suffused all of his thinking of Being from beginning to end.

7 Hebel and the Inexhaustible Depth of "Things"

Heidegger's appreciation for Hebel's poetry is not sufficiently noted. He saw in Hebel a lover of things, the poet of simple things. This is perhaps never more evident than in Heidegger's brief remarks given in appreciation for receiving the Hebel Prize at the celebration of the poet's 200th birthday held in Wiesental, 10 May 1960 (GA 16: 565–7). This little talk is hardly known, but it beautifully reveals the Heidegger that I think we must always keep in view.

Heidegger shared with his audience how he cherished Hebel's *Alemannic Poems*, the poems written in the Alemannic dialect spoken in the Swabian region. On this day, Heidegger highlighted Hebel's concern with "things," *Sachen*, and he referred to a charming poem by Hebel titled "The Summer Evening" ("*Der Sommerabend*"). The poem describes the manifold activities of the sun each day, and Heidegger made note of all the "things" that are touched by the sun in its "astonishing daily work." The sun gently illuminates the wondrous character of every particular "thing," every individual being. And he cited one line from the poem (in the Alemannic dialect):

> *Es isch e Sach, bi miner Treu,*
> *am Morge Gras und z'obe Heu!*

I render it in standard German as:

> *Es ist eine Sache, bei meiner Treu,*
> *am Morgen Gras und am Abend Heu!*

And in English translation, this reads:

> It is a thing, I do say,
> In the morning grass and evening hay!

Heidegger focused on *"e Sach"* or *"eine Sache"* – "a thing" – and he offered his audience this striking commentary:

> *e Sach* – this is to say: something astonishing because full of mystery. Insofar as no particular thing is understood on the face of it, each thing is "a thing" [that is wondrous]. Every being "has a secret door" [*het e geheimi Tür*] into the mystery, through which the being comes forth and shines forth toward us. The calling of the poet is: to point to this "secret door" in all things or even to guide us through it.

In just these few lines we learn from Heidegger, in yet another way, that there is a depth to every "thing" that cannot be exhausted by the word, even the poet's word. Every being is always *more* than what we can say or think about it. Every being is always more – it exceeds or overflows – our language and meanings.

And Heidegger underscored this by citing two lines from another poem by Hebel, "Ecstasy" (*"Ekstase"*):

> No word of language says it –
> No picture of life paints it.

The poet "brings each thing into word." Yet it is never sufficient because there always remains what is more, what Heidegger calls "the unthinkable" [*das Unausdenkbare*]:

> The unthinkable becomes present in the poetic word; it draws near to the human being.

A being is present to us in the word, but it is always more than the word. The "unthinkable" remains. There always remains the "mystery" of each and every "thing."

Similarly, there always remains the inexhaustible depth of Being itself (Beyng) – the one and unifying ontological temporal "way" (the Being-way) whereby and wherein all "things" come to be. For this very reason, Being has so many names in Heidegger's thinking, among them: *physis, aletheia,* the primordial *Logos, kosmos, hen, Ereignis,* and *Lichtung.* Furthermore, it remains our task to name Being – the inexhaustible "it" that "gives" (*Es gibt*) – yet again in our own way and in our own words. (For more on Hebel, see *Heidegger's Way of Being,* 47–9.)

8 Facticity Only in the Light of Eternity

It is arguable that every great thinker – or all genuine thinking – ultimately arrives at some kind of eternity. Heidegger is no exception. He may be the thinker of our finite "thrownness" and "facticity," but we find in his later work many reflections on Being as a *temporal* eternity or as an unending unfolding. We see this most clearly in his many later reflections on Heraclitus's fragment 30. One of his translations of the fragment reads this way:

> This *kosmos* here, insofar as it is the same for everyone and everything, no one of the gods and also no human being has brought forth; it always already was, and it is, and will be: inexhaustibly living fire, flaming up in measures, and in measures going out.
>
> (GA 15: 280)

Indeed, as I have noted earlier, in his 1944 lecture course on Heraclitus, Heidegger says of Beyng that it is "everlasting" and "on the way into its own truth" (GA 55: 345).

We must keep in mind, then, that Heidegger's thinking, properly speaking, was not limited to "finitude." We may give another example. His thinking after *Being and Time* ranged over the unending history of "epochs," what we have come to refer to in English as his "Being-historical thinking." Yet we must take into account the important implication of this thinking: It is not the case that we are trapped in our own historical "epoch" of thinking *because thought traverses all the epochs* – past, present, and those to come. We must admit that Heidegger's thinking of Being as the unending temporal *giving* (*Ereignis, Es gibt*) of all finite epochs is itself a thinking that is beyond any particular finite epoch. In other words, Heidegger's thinking of Being has an "infinite" character after all; his thinking does indeed arrive at a version of the infinite.

Consequently, if we are able to set aside the persistent biases of our day, we realize that in Heidegger's Being-historical thinking, thought transcends the finitude of any particular epoch and contemplates the whole history of epochs – and what is more, contemplates the pure "giving" of these epochs by Being itself (*Sein selbst / Seyn*). This theme of the "giving" or "sending" by Being (*das Seinsgeschick*) was most elaborately laid out by Heidegger in his 1957 text *The Principle of Ground* (*Der Satz vom Grund*, GA 10).

Therefore, we must be careful not to read Heidegger exclusively in the light of the contemporary preoccupation with "finitude" and the human being's "facticity." We must not overlook the Heidegger whose thinking was often speculative and, indeed, dare we say it, "metaphysical." Or to put this another way, his theme of the mysterious "giving" by Being of all metaphysical epochs was *itself a metaphysical speculation* – and one that was central to his lifetime of thought after *Being and Time*.

Perhaps the key lesson we learn here is that all thinking about our "facticity" must always be considered in the light of an "eternity" of some kind, just as any thinking about eternity must be held in tension with our mindfulness of our finite thrown and factical existence. Not one or the other, but both together, joined like the stretched string on Artemis's "bow," an image that Heidegger was fond of invoking. For us human beings, facticity without eternity is oppressive and unrelieved – it is the "prison" that Plato spoke of – but eternity without facticity is merely escape.

9 Another Suggestion on Thinking Heidegger and Whitehead

As I have pointed out in Chapter 6, a promising area for further research in Heidegger studies is the relation of the later Heidegger's thinking of Being and the "process" philosophical thinking of Alfred North Whitehead. Let us consider, as another example, these two observations by Whitehead in *Process and Reality* (New York: The Free Press, 1929/1978), which, if unattributed, one could very well think were composed by Heidegger:

> In the inescapable flux, there is something that abides; in the overwhelming permanence, there is an element that escapes into flux. Permanence can be snatched only out of flux; and the passing moment can find its adequate intensity only by its submission to permanence. (338)

> ... the initial intuition of permanence in fluency and fluency in permanence. (347)

As we read these, we bear in mind Heidegger's life-long discussion of Being-as-time. That is, Being unfolds beings in such a way that both the movement ("becoming") of beings and the abiding/whiling/lingering/ingathering of beings (traditionally, their "being") can be seen as but two aspects of the single temporal-spatial unfolding way that is Being itself. This was

Heidegger's – and in his own way, Whitehead's – response to the age-old traditional metaphysical distinction between becoming (potency) and being (act, actuality). In other words, this traditional distinction need not be discarded, but rather it must be *grounded* in the onefold of Being itself.

Both Heidegger and Whitehead were harsh critics of the classical metaphysics of *substance*, but at the same time they opened up new ways to think metaphysically. We are invited to think further.

This said, then, perhaps we should not be surprised that apparently Heidegger was enthusiastically receptive to a report on Whitehead's "process" thinking. Consider the following account that comes from an obscure survey article written in 1990 by Prof. Jan Van der Veken, who was a Professor of Philosophy at the *Katholieke Universiteit* Leuven and founded the European Society for Process Thought in the later 1970s. The article is titled "Process Thought from a European Perspective" (*Process Studies*, 19:4 (Winter 1990), 240). Van der Veken writes:

> In 1956, Professor John E. Smith of Yale University paid a visit to the venerable Martin Heidegger. Their conversation lasted for three hours, during which time Heidegger expressed his passionate interest in turning toward a new post-Hegelian pursuit of a philosophy of nature. Smith responded that in America A.N. Whitehead had already spawned such a movement. Heidegger was most pleasantly surprised and interested, and expressed a desire to read some of Whitehead's philosophy. It was, in fact, at Heidegger's request that the tremendous project of translating *Process and Reality* (PR) was begun at Suhrkamp Verlag (Frankfurt). However, before the translation could be made available to him, Heidegger died.

There are indeed striking similarities between the later Heidegger's thinking of Being and Whitehead's process approach, and it remains for us to consider further what may have so engaged Heidegger about Prof. Smith's prospectus on Whitehead's thought.

10 Heidegger and C.G. Jung on Wholeness as the Telos of the Human Being

Here after many hardships, endless wanderings, after twenty years,
I have come home at last.

Odyssey, XVI, 205

Too much has been written about Heidegger and Freud (especially via Lacan), and too little has been written on Heidegger and Jung. Yet Heidegger and Jung, and especially the *later* Heidegger and Jung, is a far more congenial pairing. What I highlight here – and what I hope will spur further research and discussion – is how both had in view "wholeness" or completion as the *telos* (or aim) of the human being. They both offered what we might call a descriptive phenomenology of our unfolding toward wholeness. Jung named this unfolding path "individuation," and he found the evidence in the manifold images of "wholeness" that are spontaneously generated by the human psyche. He referred to these images as "mandalas," and their distinguishing feature is the Four or Quaternity, the square and the circle. The human psyche moves and strives toward wholeness and completeness – whether the conscious ego wants to or not. Something is happening to us even without us.

It is fair to say that the early Heidegger is far from such a view. With his early emphasis on the mood of *Angst*, he represented a phenomenology of fracture that, unfortunately, has come to prevail in most Continental philosophy ever since. Yet the later

Heidegger is very different. In the later work, as I have illustrated in several places, Heidegger "turned" in his thinking to
the theme of our way back "home" in our relation to Being and
of "healing" our alienation from Being (see especially Chapters
3 and 4 of *Engaging Heidegger*). Along this later path of thinking,
he brought forth his own distinctive "mandalas" in his writings:
Being as the Fourfold; Being as "sphere," "circle," "ring," and
"center"; and indeed the joyful "ring dance" or "round dance" in
which all beings and things participate. For the later Heidegger,
as for Jung, something is happening even without us – and for
Heidegger, this is Being "calling" us "home" to ourselves and to
our relation with all things. Both Jung and the later Heidegger
took to heart the message of Homer's *Odyssey* – a message almost
completely lost in the present day – that we are making a jour-
ney, no matter how arduous, "home."

⤜ᥱᥱᥱᥱᥱᥱᥱ⤛

As a psychologist, Jung was chiefly concerned with healing the
psyche. Yet his understanding of the essence of *therapeia* differed
fundamentally from Freud's. In Jung's view, quite apart from the
resolution of unconscious personal conflicts, which was Freud's
chief concern, healing, that is, radical healing, comes with the
ego's re-cognition of the "overpowering," "numinous" collective
unconscious, which is also "truth." Jung often insisted that there
was a religious dimension to therapy, but by this he meant principally that therapy was a matter of religion, *re + ligare*, a *re-binding*
of consciousness with the unconscious process, a *re-collection*
by consciousness of the "overpowering," "unbounded," "numinous" unconscious.

Although Heidegger's concern was not properly psychological, still, his remarks on "healing" are in remarkable harmony
with Jung's. Jung named the unconscious process the "numinous," and Heidegger, especially in his commentary on Hölderlin's poetry, meditated upon Being as the Holy. Being as the Holy
is the endless temporal unfolding process that is awesome but
also *wholesome*; and the human being who dwells in nearness to
the Holy is made whole, is healed. With such healing, Heidegger

added, comes joy. Yet the joy that he spoke of is not the joy that is opposed to grief; it is the joy that comes in dwelling in nearness to the awesome unfolding of opposites – joy and grief, peace and turmoil, life and death – which is *physis*, *aletheia*, *Logos*, Being. We recall Heidegger's words from his elucidation of Hölderlin's poem "Homecoming" – words that also capture the very essence of Jung's understanding of the relation of consciousness to the unconscious:

> The original essence of joy is becoming at home in nearness to the Source.   (GA 4: 25)[1]

11 Heidegger and C.G. Jung on "Opposites"

Let us take the consideration of Heidegger and Jung one step further. Jung maintained that the unconscious is an "intelligent" structure irreducible to consciousness, and it is my suggestion that Heidegger's understanding of Being as the primordial *Logos* is helpful in elucidating Jung's position.

From within Heidegger's perspective, the term "intelligent" suggests *ontic* considerations; "intelligence" refers broadly to every which way the "metaphysical" tradition has discussed the comportment of knower to known (subject to object). Such comportment is, for Heidegger, derived from and founded upon the more fundamental openness of the human being to Being (first granted by Being to humans), whereby the human being thinks (*noein*) Being (*einai*) as the temporal unfolding process by which and through which all beings (including humans) arise and emerge. It is this ontological or fundamental thinking that grounds all ontic "intelligent" comportment of knower to known, including all "acts" of intelligence, such as the "abstraction of essences" and "judgment." For Heidegger, then, the originary coming to pass of thinking about Being is, we could say, *pre-intelligent*.

This said, it becomes clear that no easy parallel can be made between Heidegger's understanding of Being as *Logos* and Jung's understanding of the unconscious as "intelligent." Yet by more carefully considering what Jung has in mind by speaking of the unconscious as intelligent, a striking parallel can be worked out. In a section titled "Schiller's Ideas on the Type Problem," from his

1921 work *Psychological Types*, Jung argued that consciousness is not capable of preserving opposites in their original unity, since the "essence of consciousness is discrimination, distinguishing ego from non-ego, subject from object, positive from negative, and so forth."[1] "We must," he states, "appeal to another authority, where the opposites are not yet clearly separated [by conscious reflection], but still preserve their original unity." This "authority" is the unconscious: "Where purely unconscious instinctive life prevails, there is no [conscious] reflection, no pro et contra, no disunion, nothing but simple happening, where everything that is divided and antagonistic in consciousness flows together into groupings and configurations."[2]

What precisely he means by "discrimination" is not quite clear. Yet his intention appears to be that the central cognitive act of consciousness is *judgment*. One might recall that for Aristotle, in judgment distinct essences (unities, quiddities) grasped by the understanding are combined or separated (Aquinas's *compositio vel divisio*) in a statement, and the statement is either affirmed or denied; thus, for example, understanding "evenness" and understanding "oddness," the statement "the even is not the odd" is formed and judged as true.

Yet Jung further suggests that the conscious rational act of discrimination (judgment) is derivative. At a deeper level of thinking, we are aware that the unconscious "happens" as opposites. The unconscious allows what is generally separated or opposed in the judgment to "happen" together, and, moreover, this "happening" is a patterning, for as Jung observes, the unconscious appears to pattern opposites into "groupings and configurations." It is this patterning of opposites that, at least in part, informs Jung's position that the unconscious is "intelligent." Put another way, for Jung, the essential *logos* of rational consciousness (judgment) is derived from and founded upon the more fundamental *logos* of the unconscious that lets opposites happen and maintains them in tension. It is only because the unconscious "happens" as opposites that opposites can be "discriminated" in consciousness (judgment).

꒰ꙮ꒱

Therefore, it is this understanding of "intelligent" that draws Jung's understanding of the unconscious closer to Heidegger's understanding of Being as the primordial *Logos*. In *Introduction to Metaphysics*, Heidegger argues that by *logos* the early Greeks named Being as the "primal gathering principle" or "the original unifying unity of what tends apart."[3] He adds that as "Heraclitus says in fragment 8: "Opposites move back and forth, the one to the other; from out of themselves, they gather themselves. The conflict of the opposites is a gathering, rooted in togetherness; it is *logos*."[4] In another passage he observes, "Therefore Being, the *logos*, as gathering and harmony, ... is unlike the harmony that is mere compromise, destruction of tension, flattening."[5] Further, Being as *logos* "does not let what it holds in its power dissolve into an empty freedom from opposition, but by unifying the opposites maintains the full sharpness of their tension."[6]

Consequently, for Heidegger, Being, as the primordial *Logos*, simultaneously lets lie and gathers together beings in their correlative opposition. Being lets opposites "happen." Therefore, a distinctively Heideggerian response to the traditional Aristotelian position might be articulated in this way: In the "not" of the proposition "the even is not the odd" lies concealed "nothing," no-thing, Being, the primordial *Logos* that lets the even and the odd come to presence as opposites. Only because Being happens as opposites can opposites be subsequently separated in judgment. The task of thinking, then, is to think Being, not principally ontically (abstraction and judgment), but ontologically as the *Logos*, as No-thing, which lays out opposites and gathers them together. As he remarks provocatively in the essay "Nihilism as Determined by the History of Being": "Ascent versus decline, waxing versus waning, exaltation versus degradation, construction versus destruction, all play their roles as counterphenomena in the realm of beings.... Being applies to the essence of nihilism, since Being itself has brought it to pass in history that there is nothing to Being itself."[7]

In *Introduction to Metaphysics*, he also argues in another way that Being happens as opposites. He maintains that the traditional Aristotelian understanding of unity as "self-sameness" is derivative of the more primordial understanding of Being as the

Hen (One) that lets all beings be: "In speaking of Being, the unity must be understood as Parmenides understood the word *Hen*. We know that this unity is never empty indifference; it is not sameness in the sense of mere equivalence. Unity is the belonging together of antagonisms. This is original oneness."[8]

In the essay "*Logos* (Heraclitus, B 50)," he elaborates on this theme. He gives a highly novel interpretation of the Greek expression *Hen-Panta*, the One and the Many. "*Hen-Panta* is not what *Logos* pronounces," he states; "rather, *Hen-Panta* names the way in which *Logos* essentially unfolds."[9] In other words, *Hen-Panta* names Being as the temporal unfolding process: *Hen* names the One as Being as the unfolding itself by which all beings are let be, and *Panta* (Many) names the ensemble of beings that are let be by the One as the unifying, gathering unfolding process. The crucial point is reached, however, when Heidegger further observes that the *Hen* unfolds as *Panta*, as opposites. He remarks in a particularly incisive – and poetic – way that:

> We can see in *Logos* how the *Hen* essentially occurs as unifying....
> The *Hen-Panta* lets lie together before us in one presencing things which are usually separated from, and opposed to, one another, such as day and night, winter and summer, peace and war, waking and sleeping, Dionysus and Hades. Such opposites, borne along the farthest distance between presence and absence, *diapheromenon*, let the laying that gathers lie before us in its full bearing. Its laying is itself that which carries things along by bearing them out. The *Hen* is itself a carrying out.[10]

Central to Heidegger's thinking is this notion that Being as the primordial *Logos* lets lie and gathers together beings in their respective opposition. It is this position that is helpful in elucidating Jung's understanding of the unconscious as an "intelligent" structure irreducible to consciousness. Again in the essay on the *Logos* of Heraclitus, Heidegger notes that to lay is also to gather (*lesen*) and adds, "The *lesen* better known to us, namely, the reading of something written, remains but one sort of gathering, in the sense of bringing-together-into-lying-before, although it is indeed the predominant sort."[11]

It is along these lines, then, that we may best understand Jung's position that the unconscious is "intelligent." In other words, the Jungian unconscious is understandable in terms of *intelligere* (from the Latin *legere*, to read) as the "reading" that is a laying and gathering of beings in their correlative opposition, and not in terms of the *intelligere* of the classical metaphysical tradition which is the "reading" into beings, that is, the penetration to the "essence" of things and the formation of judgments. This classical metaphysical understanding of *intelligere* is perhaps best articulated by Aquinas, who states in *De Veritate* that "to understand (*intelligere*) means to read what is inside a thing (*intus legere*). The intellect alone penetrates to the interior and to the essence of a thing."[12]

Finally, then, the significance of Jung's position opens up to us. According to Jung, the unconscious as "truth" "realizes" itself through the "medium" of consciousness. In what way it may be said that the unconscious is "truth" now comes into focus: The "collective" unconscious discloses itself to consciousness as the process which lets opposites "happen." It is this "truth" which is "realized" through consciousness. By turning to Heidegger we are able to draw out the full significance of this Jungian position; that is, we are able to make more sense of Jung's speaking of the unconscious process that lets opposites happen – the "*logos*" of the unconscious – as the "truth" of the unconscious. Thus, in the essay on Heraclitus's *Logos*, Heidegger observes that Being as the *primordial Logos* is also named *primordial truth – aletheia*:

> Because the *Logos* lets lie before us what lies before us as such, it discloses what is present in its presencing. But disclosure is *aletheia*. *Aletheia* and *Logos* are the Same.[13]

In sum, then, for Heidegger, Being-as-*Logos*-as-*aletheia* is the *Hen*, the One, from out of which all "opposites" unfold and flow forth, and Jung ultimately arrived at a similar position in his late work *Mysterium Coniunctionis*. He came to affirm that beyond even the collective unconscious there must be, in the language of the alchemists, an *unus mundus*, a numinous and mysterious "one world," which is the unifying "Source" of all opposites.[14]

12 Heidegger and Melville

Heidegger cited Herman Melville in at least one place. In *Heidegger's Way of Being*, I made a point of reading Heidegger in the light of American authors such as Whitman, Emerson, Muir, and e.e. cummings (as well as English poets such as Wordsworth and Hopkins). We are not limited to Heidegger's preference for Hölderlin and other German poets in elucidating Heidegger's central themes.

In his *Black Notebooks* (GA 97), Heidegger cites one line from *Moby-Dick* as an epigraph on a cover page, dated 1948. The line is quoted in German, and it seems that Heidegger was familiar only with the German translation of this great American novel. I say this because the German line cited says something slightly different from the original. Heidegger quotes the line this way:

Eine schöne Menschenstirn in Gedanken gleicht dem Osten, in dem der Morgen dämmert.

We may translate this as: "A fine human brow in thought is like the East in which the morning dawns."

But here is Melville's line, which we find in *Moby-Dick*, Chapter LXXXIX (79), *The Prairie*:

In thought, a fine human brow is like the East when troubled with the morning.

If Heidegger were familiar with the original, we might assume that he would have taken note of Melville's word "troubled." Nevertheless, it is possible that Heidegger did know the original but was simply more attracted to the more serene German translation. We are left wondering.

In any case, here is the rest of Melville's remarkable reflection, which resonates with the concerns of the later Heidegger in at least three ways: (1) the primacy of Being in relation to the human being; (2) honoring the inexhaustibility and thus the "mystery" of Being as *aletheia* and *physis* as emergence; and (3) coming to respect and abide by the *limit* of our ability to "read" (to make sense of) all that gathers and presents itself. In fact, we should not at all be surprised that Heidegger found a kindred spirit in Melville. Consider Melville's cautionary lines in full:

> In thought, a fine human brow is like the East when troubled with the morning. In the repose of the pasture, the curled brow of the bull has a touch of the grand in it. Pushing heavy cannon up mountain defiles, the elephant's brow is majestic. Human or animal, the mystical brow is as that great golden seal affixed by the German emperors to their decrees. It signifies – 'God: done this day by my hand.' But in most creatures, nay in man himself, very often the brow is but a mere strip of alpine land lying along the snow-line. Few are the foreheads which like Shakespeare's or Melanchthon's rise so high, and descend so low, that the eyes themselves seem clear, eternal, tideless mountain lakes; and all above them in the forehead's wrinkles, you seem to track the antlered thoughts descending there to drink, as the Highland hunters track the snow-prints of the deer. But in the great sperm whale, this high and mighty god-like dignity inherent in the brow is so immensely amplified, that gazing on it, in that full front view, you feel the Deity and the dread powers more forcibly than in beholding any other object in living nature. For you see no one point precisely; not one distinct feature is revealed; no nose, eyes, ears, or mouth; no face; he has none, proper; nothing but that one broad firmament of a forehead, plaited with riddles; dumbly lowering with the doom of boats, and ships, and men. Nor, in profile, does this wondrous brow diminish; though that way viewed its grandeur

does not domineer upon you so. In profile, you plainly perceive that horizontal, semi-crescentic depression in the forehead's middle, which, in man, is Lavater's mark of genius.

But how? Genius in the sperm whale? Has the sperm whale ever written a book, spoken a speech? No, his great genius is declared in his doing nothing particular to prove it. It is moreover declared in his pyramidical silence. And this reminds me that had the great sperm whale been known to the young Orient world, he would have been deified by their child-magician thoughts. They deified the crocodile of the Nile, because the crocodile is tongueless; and the sperm whale has no tongue, or at least it is so exceedingly small, as to be incapable of protrusion. If hereafter any highly cultured, poetical nation shall lure back to their birthright, the merry May-day gods of old; and livingly enthrone them again in the now egotistical sky; in the now unhaunted hill; then be sure, exalted to Jove's high seat, the great sperm whale shall lord it.

Champollion deciphered the wrinkled granite hieroglyphics. But there is no Champollion to decipher the Egypt of every man's and every being's face. Physiognomy, like every other human science, is but a passing fable. If then, Sir William Jones, who read in thirty languages, could not read the simplest peasant's face in its profounder and more subtle meanings, how may unlettered Ishmael hope to read the awful Chaldee of the sperm whale's brow? I but put that brow before you. *Read it if you can.*

13 Heidegger and a Robert Frost Poem

We may also look to the poetry of Robert Frost to amplify Heidegger's thinking of Being. Take, for example, Frost's poem "Gathering Leaves." Much can be said, but just a few comments to get us thinking. Here is the third stanza of the poem:

But the mountains I raise
Elude my embrace,
Flowing over my arms
And into my face.

Frost reminds us that our "gathering" of leaves – even "mountains" of them – is limited; there is always "more" of Nature that "eludes" our embrace, that "flows over" our effort to gather it into language and comprehension. Nature "faces" us again and again with its newness and freshness. We recall that for Heidegger Being as *physis* (as Nature) always "exceeds" the meanings we "gather." There is a depth to Being that is never exhausted by our words and meanings.

Also consider Frost's last stanza of the poem that reflects on the outcome of our hard work to "gather" the leaves:

Next to nothing for use,
But a crop is a crop,
And who's to say where
The harvest shall stop?

What is the point of the "gathering" that we work at between birth and death? Maybe not much in the long run, but "a crop is a crop" after all. That is, a life is a life, we might say, and there is satisfaction in just that. We can come to accept our "crop." In Heidegger's words, finally, we "release" (*Gelassenheit*) ourselves to what "is."

But here is the kicker: Frost raises the possibility that the "gathering" will go on – a "harvest" after death? Heidegger's way is to remain open to the Being-way. We pass in and we pass away, and we "gather" what we can along the way. That's quite enough we might say. But the "mystery" of Being calls upon us to remain open and in wonder. So, we may say that for Heidegger, too, "who's to say where the harvest shall stop?"

14 The Unspeakable Mystery of All Things

GA 100, a recently published volume in the *Black Notebooks* series, opens with Heidegger offering (dated 1952/53) a characteristic reflection that once again reminds us of the inadequacy of all pragmatic, transcendental-phenomenological, analytic, and biographical-sociological-political readings of his thinking of Being. It also reminds us of how Heidegger continued to use elements of his Catholic upbringing and milieu (in this case the "vigil day" and the color blue of the priest's "chasuble")[1] to point to the unspeakable depth and mystery of things. His recollection:

> In my youth, the vigil days, the days *before* the high feast days, were the most mysterious; they enchanted all expectations, and yet they placed everything into stillness, that which draws back into itself. The blue color of the chasubles on these days gathered everything into an inexplicable depth. The feast day itself seemed then almost as if empty and overly noisy and drawn into the public eye. No one respected the vigil. Presumably because we can hardly measure how it is that all true and inviolable treasure of mortals rests in the unattained, in the granting of the ever *veiled* gift.[2]

(GA 100: 9, my translation, Heidegger's italics)

15 A "Hermetic Saying" and the Hermetic Tradition

In the most recently published volume of the *Black Notebooks* (GA 101 *Winke I und II*), Heidegger opens his reflections (or "hints," *Winke*) in 1957 with several citations, and one is especially curious – and perhaps telling. It is a quote that is well known as a characterization of "God," especially in the Hermetic traditions broadly understood. He cites in Latin what he refers to as a "Hermetic saying" (*Hermetischer Spruch*):

> Sphaera infinita, cuius centrum
> ubique, circumferentia nusquam est.

> [An] infinite sphere whose center is everywhere
> and whose circumference is nowhere.

What is Heidegger "hinting" at by citing this "saying"? Let us first acknowledge that this citation once again reveals to us the Heidegger that many contemporary readings completely miss. As I have remarked many times before, we must keep this Heidegger in view.

This "Hermetic saying" was well known as a "definition" or characterization of "God" in the philosophical, religious, and mystical traditions. There remains scholarly debate about whether this "saying" reaches back to the ancient world. Many have claimed that it goes back to Aristotle, or even earlier among the Greeks. Others point back in particular to the fourth century

Roman Neoplatonic thinker Marius Victorinus, who, among other things, translated two of Aristotle's books into Latin. Such discussions continue. Nevertheless, it is well documented that this "sentence" or "definition" appeared in Latin manuscripts in the Middle Ages from as early as the twelfth century with the title *Liber viginti quattuor philosophorum*,[1] or in English, *Book of Twenty-Four Philosophers*.

This Book was admired by many in the Middle Ages and in later centuries as well, and it influenced a number of philosophers, theologians, and mystics. Some even believed that it was authored by the mysterious ancient figure of Hermes Trismegistus, the legendary "founder" of the "Hermetic" tradition of thinking and practice.

What we have of this "Book" is really only a series of short statements in Latin concerning the nature of God. The *Liber* opens with a Prologue that states that twenty-four philosophers were brought together to discuss all kinds of matters and that one question remained for them: *quid est Deus*? (*What is God?*) What follows in the manuscript are the twenty-four "answers" to this question. Heidegger's citation in GA 101 corresponds to the second of these characterizations. We may dig deeper to determine whether Heidegger ever referred to the *Liber* explicitly, but what we do know – and what is so intriguing – is that he was clearly aware that this statement was part of the Hermetic tradition. Let us not forget: He cited the line as a "*Hermetischer Spruch*," a "Hermetic saying."

Consequently, certain questions arise: In what way might the Hermetic tradition have influenced Heidegger's understanding of Being and of the "relation" between Being and the human being? Is Heidegger's citation of the "Hermetic saying" his indication, his clue, his hint (*Wink*) that he was in sympathy with the Hermetic tradition's emphasis on the immediate "relation" of God and the human being? Is it a hint that the Hermetic view may have been one spur to his own effort to rethink the "relation" of Being and the human being so as to recover the mysterious "oneness" of that "relation"?

Let us consider further. This particular "saying" has been discussed by certain scholars in other contexts. For example, some have argued that the characterization of God as "infinite sphere" was important in the history of ideas insofar as it helped pave the way to modern conceptions of an "infinite" cosmos. These are interesting studies, but this is not the influence on Heidegger's thinking that is apparent or decisive.

Rather, it would appear that the primary influence of the Hermetic tradition on Heidegger's thought had to do with their understanding of the closeness or immediacy of the relation of God and the human being. That is, it was the Hermetic celebration and cultivation of the experience of God "within" the human soul that was decisive: the "divinization" of the human being, we may say. We know that Heidegger turned away from the scholastic Catholicism of his youth, in part because that religious tradition was too much about "externals" – dogma, doctrine, and ritual – and not enough about the personal or "inner" experience of God. The God of scholasticism is too distant and removed from the human being.

Of course, Heidegger was not concerned with the experience of "God" as such, since the term "God" was simply too freighted as it was passed down in the Christian, and particularly Catholic, intellectual tradition. Yet let us keep in mind that Heidegger *was* always concerned with *the experience of Being*. He wanted to recover the earliest Greek experience of Being, as he emphasized again and again, because there was an immediacy, intensity, and vibrancy in their relation to Being. In Heidegger's grand narrative, this originary experience of Being was largely lost in the subsequent epochs of Western thinking and culture. Being was "forgotten," to recall his famous formulation.

What the alternative Hermetic tradition offered Heidegger, especially as it came down to him through the Christian thinking of Meister Eckhart and Jakob Böhme, was perhaps the echo of the originary experience of Being among the earliest Greeks that so fascinated him. The basic Hermetic idea that we humans must peel back the many layers of the self to uncover the presence of the divine – or even to recognize our own "divinity" – was recast by Heidegger into his own fundamental theme of our need to strip away the many layers of philosophical and theological thought in order to revivify the experience of Being. In his talk, "Poverty" ("*Die Armut*," 1945), he characterized "the spiritual" as the "concentrated" relationship of Beyng and the "human essence," and he invoked this very same statement about the "circle" – but without citing the *Liber* or citing the line as a "Hermetic saying." Still, in typical Hermetic fashion, Heidegger added that this understanding of the relationship of Beyng and the human being is "intimated by *only a few*" (GA 73.1: 877, my emphasis).

Furthermore, it is in this context that we can perhaps make the most sense of Heidegger's affinity for Heraclitus's fragment 45 (GA 55: 282ff.; see also my *Heidegger's Way of Being*, Chapter 6):

ψυχῆς πείρατα ἰὼν οὐκ ἂν ἐξεύροιο πᾶσαν ἐπιπορευόμενος ὁδόν· οὕτω βαθὺν λόγον ἔχει

This fragment is generally translated into English along the lines of:

Traveling on every path, you will not find the boundaries of soul in any direction – so deep is its measure.

We should not be surprised that this fragment of Heraclitus was taken up in the Hermetic traditions. It seems evident that Heidegger resonated with this Heraclitean/Hermetic theme that the "relation" of Being and the human being is ultimately a mysterious and unsayable "oneness" – precisely what, in his view, traditional Christian metaphysics and theology was unable or unwilling to recognize. As with Hermetic thinkers of one kind or another over the many centuries, Heidegger, in his own way and using his own language, endeavored to affirm and preserve the primacy of Being while at the same time revealing the seamlessness of our essential "relation" to Being. Indeed, through this interpretive lens, many of Heidegger's own enigmatic "sayings," such as we find in his elucidations of Heraclitus, come into better focus:

Being itself can in no way be grasped like a thing or an object, not because it still remains too distant from the human, but rather because it has already come too close to the human.

(GA 55: 293)

꧁꧂

My observations here are intended only as "hints" (*Winke*), as Heidegger would say, that may help us better understand and appreciate the fundamental motifs of his thinking. It has been largely overlooked in the Heidegger scholarship that the Hermetic tradition played *some* part in the development and unfolding of his thinking. These reflections point the way toward further consideration.

16 Heidegger and Walt Whitman

In my Acknowledgments to *Heidegger's Way of Being*, I concluded with a dedication to Walt Whitman, "to the singer of the songs I have always heard most vividly, perhaps because I, too, started from Paumanok." I recently returned to Paumanok (Long Island, New York), where I was born and grew up, to visit with old friends. "Paumanok" was one of the names given to the "fish-shaped" land by the Native Americans who dwelled there, and it was a name that Whitman cherished. "Paumanok" means roughly "land of tribute," and it is especially apt when considering Whitman's poetic celebration of both nature and city. *Everything* gives tribute to the mysterious motion and spirit that rolls through all things – what Heidegger, philosophically and also poetically, named Being as *physis* and as *aletheia*.

My return to Whitman's birthplace home in Huntington, Long Island, brought home to me once again the beautiful spiritual vision of Whitman's poetry – but also of Heidegger's thinking. They share a vision that is not "identical" but "the Same," to use one of Heidegger's favorite turns of phrase. In other words, we can hear Whitman's voice when, for example, Heidegger speaks of all things as "ensouled" and "breathing in and out" along with Being (GA 55: 280). Or again when Heidegger remarks (GA 15: 282) that Being as *physis* as *kosmos* "shimmers ungraspably through everything."

Astonishingly, there is a secret at the heart of things that is the source of joy for us.

17 Heidegger and the Limit of Language – and Rumi

The turn to "language" in Continental philosophy in the latter part of the twentieth century brought with it peculiar philosophical conclusions. For example, it became fashionable to make the claim that what "is" – being – is reducible to language; that is, "being" (or "Being" when I refer to Heidegger's understanding of *Sein* or *Seyn*) is constituted and measured out by human language. I have discussed the philosophical difficulties with this proposition in other places, and here I am more concerned to point out that it is a mistake to consider this to be Heidegger's position on language. Those in Continental thinking who continue to view language in this way often look to Heidegger as the principal progenitor of the position, yet what has been thereby overlooked is how Heidegger in fact rejected a reduction of Being to language. Indeed, he insisted that Being always exceeds language and remains beyond the reach – and capture – of language. (See also *Heidegger's Way of Being*, especially Chapter 3.)

Heidegger's text often cited by those who maintain the reduction of being to language is "The Essence of Language" ("*Das Wesen der Sprache*," 1957–8, GA 12, 149–204), and in English translation, in *On the Way to Language* (OWL), trans. Peter Hertz, Harper & Row, 1971, 57–108). In particular, they cite the conclusion of the text, where Heidegger invokes the poet Stefan George's line: "Where the word breaks off no thing may be" (GA 12: 204; OWL:108). The problem is that they do not take into account what follows. Heidegger immediately proceeds to cite the line "An 'is' arises where the word breaks up." In other words, he is concerned to show that the "is" – Being – reveals itself as what is *beyond* language, what exceeds, overflows, evades language, what is *inexpressible*. As Heidegger puts it, "the sounding word returns into the soundlessness, back to whence it was granted: into the ringing of stillness." That is, the word is but an echo of the Source, and our most proper comportment to Being is – *silence*.

Heidegger reiterated this theme throughout his later work (see my previous reflection on Hebel, for example), and yet somehow it is missed by those who maintain the reduction of being to language and make Heidegger their champion.

The key point to be made here is this: Although Heidegger cherished language and especially poetic language, and although he was intensely interested in uncovering and recovering the deeper nature of language, still, he never proffered the position that Being is reducible to language. In fact, quite to the contrary, he resisted all such reductions and made it his life's work to "free" and "safeguard" Being from human capture.

It seems, then, that what is so difficult to accept for many scholars and commentators in the contemporary age is that Heidegger belongs to a long tradition of poets and thinkers who have understood that the Source of all human language and meaning is *beyond* all human language and meaning. The Source is expressed by us again and again, and yet it remains *inexpressible*. Heidegger highlighted this in his reflections on Hölderlin's poem "Homecoming." Being as the Holy reaches human beings especially through the poet's words, but the poet's words can never exhaust the Holy as "the Source" (*der Ursprung*). The best that we human beings can do is draw near to the Source and dwell in nearness to the Source ("homecoming"), but we can never penetrate the ultimate mystery of the Source. As he put it explicitly in his commentary: "we must preserve the mystery as mystery" (GA 4: 24). This is the fundamental matter that always concerned Heidegger in all of his signature formulations: Being as *physis* both shows itself and hides itself. Being as *aletheia* reveals itself and conceals itself.

Being as the Source shines forth and yet maintains itself in reserve. Being is named and yet remains nameless. Being is "mystery" (*das Geheimnis*).

Almost fifty years after Heidegger's death, it is time for scholars and commentators – for all readers – to recognize that Heidegger *shared* in a longstanding view, stretching across the ages and across world cultures, that the Source is manifested by language but not exhausted by language. He recalled and restated this insight for us. To be sure, he did so in an original and creative way, but, admittedly, it is unfortunate that he put so great a distance between himself and other authors past and present. He too often disowned a distinctive tradition of thinking that he was part of nevertheless. As Heidegger scholarship moves forward, it would be benefited by recognizing and accepting this and not persisting in claiming a radical "overcoming" of all past traditions of thinking.

I have brought Heidegger into proximity to several other poets, thinkers, and authors, and in this reflection let us listen especially to the testimony of the great Persian poet Rumi. There are many beautiful and evocative poems that we could consider, but just a few lines will suffice (from *The Essential Rumi* [ER], trans. Coleman Barks [New York: HarperCollins, 2004]). In the last stanza of the poem, "This World Which Is Made of Our Love for Emptiness," the poet comes to the realization that the words used in the poem fail to capture their Source:

> These words I'm saying begin to lose meaning:
> existence, emptiness, mountain, straw: words
> and what they try to say swept
> out the window, down the slant of the roof.   (ER: 22)

Ultimately, we learn that not words but *silence* is most befitting before the great mystery. We must be awakened to a new life capable of silence, unlike our "old life," about which Rumi says in another poem: "Your old life was a frantic running from silence" (ER: 22).

Centuries before Heidegger, Rumi understood that even the poet's language is not enough. The Source surpasses. In the poem "A Thirsty Fish," Rumi ruefully but also humorously remarks:

This is how it always is
when I finish a poem.
A great silence overcomes me,
and I wonder why I ever thought
to use language.   (ER: 20)

Ah, if only Heidegger had this light touch of Rumi!

18 Thomas Aquinas, "God," and the "Godhead of God"

To return to the *Black Notebooks* and GA 100 (covering the years 1952–7), one is struck by the high "mysticism" of many of Heidegger's reflections on Being (Beyng) and on "God."

One matter that emerges clearly in this volume is that Heidegger kept up his sharp criticism of a metaphysics of substance – and of Thomas Aquinas. Heidegger's quarrel was principally with a metaphysics of substance, and in GA 100, he again put it in the crosshairs.

For example, Heidegger criticizes the understanding of God as the "overarching cause" of all beings (37). In any such metaphysical scheme, he observes, the "divinity of God" (*die Göttlichkeit des Gottes*) is obscured or eclipsed altogether, and the very "Godhead of God" (*die Gottheit des Gottes*) is denied its "free region of shining forth." (He made similar remarks in the 1957 lecture "The Onto-theo-logical Constitution of Metaphysics," GA 11: 77.) According to Heidegger, this loss of "the divine God" (*das göttliche Gott*) is the consequence of the kind of metaphysics that underlies the tradition of a "rational natural theology," and he goes so far as to say that this metaphysics and theology of God as the "highest cause" "pays homage to *the purest atheism*" (*dem reinsten Atheismus*). This is a provocative claim (and no doubt a debatable one). Of course, this is not the first time (nor the last time) that Heidegger levied such a charge against this kind of theology; nevertheless, it is of interest that we find this stinging criticism in this volume as well.

Yet what is more instructive is that in another reflection, Heidegger challenges *"Thomas von Aquin"* more directly. Heidegger notes (226) that according to Aquinas, God cannot do what is contradictory; that is, "God stands under the law of non-contradiction." Heidegger objects to this by asking one decisive and devastating question:

> And whoever argues as Thomas does – does he not believe even more in the principle of contradiction than in God?

Apparently, in Heidegger's view, "the divine God" should not be said to "stand under the law of non-contradiction." More broadly, what he appears to reject is Aquinas's *analogical* understanding of God; that is, Heidegger's utterly mysterious "divine God" is *not* subject to our rational constraints – including the foundational rational principle of non-contradiction. In such passages, Heidegger seems to weigh in on the side of Protestant Christian thinkers like Karl Barth against the long Catholic intellectual tradition of *analogia entis*.

Yet we need not venture too far into such a discussion here. The point is that various reflections in GA 100 underscore Heidegger's life-long critique of scholastic metaphysics and theology. Nonetheless, as I have pointed out, we should also keep in mind that Heidegger did retain in his thinking many elements of his Catholic upbringing and milieu, but he often transformed these elements into "gateways" to reflection on ultimate *mystery*.

~ᕲᕲᕲ~

"Mystery," *"Geheimnis,"* is certainly one of Heidegger's essential words. In fact, we may say that his foremost concern, especially in his later work, was to safeguard the unfathomable mystery of Being.

Thus one central lesson to be learned from the later Heidegger's thinking of Being is this: In the hyper-humanism of our times – along with its accompanying manifold forms of closure – our task is to remain *open* to ultimate mystery.

Afterword

Poetry *implies* the whole truth. Philosophy *expresses* a particle of it.

Henry David Thoreau, Journal entry, 1852

In Heidegger studies, we must be on guard not to claim too much for Heidegger's thinking. It is perfectly appropriate to acknowledge and even to celebrate the creativity and originality of his thought, but it is too much to say that it is without precedent or that it does not dovetail in significant ways the thought of other thinkers and poets across the ages and across cultures. Heidegger's language is distinctive, to be sure, but this does not mean that what he labored a lifetime to bring to language was not also in the sight and word of others. In fact, one of the great satisfactions of studying Heidegger's thought is that we come to recognize in his vision the comparable vision of others past and present – and also that we may come to recognize and affirm our own vision of how things are and give it expression, perhaps for the first time.

When we realize that there really is nothing new under the sun, then we are liberated to follow Heidegger's path of thinking all the way, every step of it, without the illusion that only he saw the fundamental matter or that only his language can say it. There is freedom but also delight and joy in our seeing it and saying it again, whether with the words and images of others or with our own deeply personal and private expressions. Heidegger is our guide, not our master.

And so we come back to Heidegger's vision of Being. In *Engaging Heidegger, Heidegger's Way of Being*, and now in this present volume, I have made every effort to attend to the smallest details of his texts in order to draw out the larger picture of his thinking of Being. Being as unfolding-as-Nature is but one of his manifold ways of articulating the core matter. In something as simple as the sound of the dry leaves of Autumn dancing their way across the ground in the gentle breeze, there is the opening to the Being-way, namely, that which moves in and through all things, that which unfolds and enfolds all things.

Heidegger opened our eyes to this "hidden" or "inapparent" source and flow of all things, which also unveils itself as "holy" and "divine." He brought us far along this way, but we need to remain open to hear all who discern the Being-way in the simplest of the simple things of this "shimmering *kosmos*." In my American New England setting, I hear, for example, the words of Thoreau from his journal in 1855:

> I go across Walden. My shadow is very blue. It is especially blue when there is a bright sunlight on pure white snow. It suggests that there may be something divine, something celestial, in me.

But, now, fellow traveler, what words do *you* hear to say "the Same"?

A Note on the Text and Heidegger's *Gesamtausgabe*

I use the convention of writing Heidegger's "Being" with a capital "B." This is an orthographical convention in the English-language Heidegger scholarship that goes back to the late 1950s and early 1960s and is followed here. The capital "B" "Being" was employed by the late preeminent Heidegger scholar William J. Richardson in his groundbreaking commentary *Heidegger: Through Phenomenology to Thought* (Kluwer), first published in 1963. Yet he was certainly not alone in employing this convention, and over the years many other eminent commentators and translators have found the convention useful. For a discussion of the philosophical intentions and justifications for this convention, see Chapter 3 of this book.

All references in the book to Heidegger's *Gesamtausgabe* ("Collected Works") cite the volume and page in this form: (GA + volume number: page number), as I also indicate in the chapter endnotes. What follows is a comprehensive (but not yet complete) bibliographical list of the published volumes in the *Gesamtausgabe*.

Martin Heidegger's Gesamtausgabe *published by Vittorio Klostermann, Frankfurt am Main*

GA 1. *Frühe Schriften* (1912–16). Ed. Friedrich-Wilhelm von Herrmann, 1978.

GA 2. *Sein und Zeit* (1927). Ed. Friedrich Wilhelm von Herrmann, 1977.

GA 3. *Kant und das Problem der Metaphysik* (1929). Ed. Friedrich-Wilhelm von Herrmann, 1991.

GA 4. *Erläuterungen zu Hölderlins Dichtung* (1936–68). Ed. Friedrich-Wilhelm von Herrmann, 1981, 2012 (rev. ed.).

GA 5. *Holzwege* (1935–46). Ed. Friedrich-Wilhelm von Hermann, 1977.

GA 6.2 *Nietzsche II* (1939–46). Ed. Brigitte Schillbach, 1997.

GA 7. *Vorträge und Aufsätze* (1936–53). Ed. Friedrich-Wilhelm von Herrmann, 2000.

GA 8. *Was heißt Denken?* (1951–2). Ed. Paola-Ludovika Coriando, 2002.

GA 9. *Wegmarken* (1919–61). Ed. Friedrich-Wilhelm von Herrmann, 1976, 1996 (rev. ed.).

GA 10. *Der Satz vom Grund* (1957). Ed. Petra Jaeger, 1997.

GA 11. *Identität und Differenz* (1955–63). Ed. Friedrich-Wilhelm von Herrmann, 2006.

GA 12. *Unterwegs zur Sprache* (1950–9). Ed. Friedrich-Wilhelm von Herrmann, 1985.

GA 13. *Aus der Erfahrung des Denkens* (1910–76). Ed. Hermann Heidegger, 1983, 2002 (rev. ed.).

GA 14. *Zur Sache des Denkens* (1927–68). Ed. Friedrich-Wilhelm von Herrmann, 2007.

GA 16. *Reden und andere Zeugnisse eines Lebensweges* (1910–76). Ed. Hermann Heidegger, 2000.

GA 18. *Grundbegriffe der aristotelischen Philosophie* (1924). Ed. Mark Michalski, 2002.

GA 19. *Platon: Sophistes* (1924–5). Ed. Ingeborg Schüßler, 1992.

GA 20. *Prolegomena zur Geschichte des Zeitbegriffs* (1925). Ed. Petra Jaeger, 1979, 1988 (2nd, rev. ed.), 1994 (3rd, rev. ed.).

GA 21. *Logik. Die Frage nach der Wahrheit* (1925–6). Ed. Walter Biemel, 1976, 1995 (rev. ed.).

GA 24. *Die Grundprobleme der Phänomenologie* (1927). Ed. Friedrich-Wilhelm von Herrmann, 1975.

GA 25. *Phänomenologische Interpretation von Kants Kritik der reinen Vernunft* (1927–8). Ed. Ingtraud Görland, 1977.

GA 26. *Metaphysische Anfangsgründe der Logik im Ausgang von Leibniz* (1928). Ed. Klaus Held, 1978, 1990 (2nd rev. ed.), 2007 (3rd rev. ed.).

GA 27. *Einleitung in die Philosophie* (1928–9). Ed. Otto Saame and Ina Saame-Speidel, 1996, 2001 (rev. ed.).

GA 28. *Der deutsche Idealismus (Fichte, Schelling, Hegel) und die philosophische Problemlage der Gegenwart* (1929). Ed. Claudius Strube, 1997.

GA 29/30. *Die Grundbegriffe der Metaphysik. Welt – Endlichkeit – Einsamkeit* (1929–30). Ed. Friedrich-Wilhelm von Herrmann, 1983.

GA 31. *Vom Wesen der menschlichen Freiheit. Einleitung in die Philosophie* (1930). Ed. Hartmut Tietjen, 1982, 1994 (rev. ed.).

GA 32. *Hegels Phänomenologie des Geistes* (1930–1). Ed. Ingtraud Görland, 1980.

GA 33. *Aristoteles, Metaphysik Θ 1–3. Von Wesen und Wirklichkeit der Kraft* (1931). Ed. Heinrich Hüni, 1981, 1990 (2nd rev. ed.), 2006 (3rd rev. ed.).

GA 34. *Vom Wesen der Wahrheit. Zu Platons Höhlengleichnis und Theätet* (1931–2). Ed. Hermann Mörchen, 1988, 1997 (rev. ed.).

GA 35. *Der Anfang der abendländischen Philosophie: Auslegung des Anaximander und Parmenides* (1932). Ed. Peter Trawny, 2011.

GA 36/37. *Sein und Wahrheit* (1933–4). Ed. Hartmut Tietjen, 2001.

GA 38. *Logik als die Frage nach dem Wesen der Sprache* (1934). Ed. Günter Seubold, 1998.

GA 39. *Hölderlins Hymnen "Germanien" und "Der Rhein"* (1934–5). Ed. Susanne Ziegler, 1980, 1989 (rev. ed.).

GA 40. *Einführung in die Metaphysik* (1935). Ed. Petra Jaeger, 1983.

GA 41. *Die Frage nach dem Ding. Zu Kants Lehre von den transzendentalen Grundsätzen* (1935–6). Ed. Petra Jaeger, 1984.

GA 42. *Schelling: Vom Wesen der menschlichen Freiheit (1809)* (1936). Ed. Ingrid Schüßler, 1988.

GA 43. *Nietzsche: Der Wille zur Macht als Kunst* (1936–7). Ed. Bernd Heimbüchel, 1985.

GA 44. *Nietzsches metaphysische Grundstellung im abendländischen Denken: Die ewige Wiederkehr des Gleichen* (1937). Ed. Marion Heinz, 1986.

GA 45. *Grundfragen der Philosophie. Ausgewählte "Probleme" der "Logik"* (1937–8). Ed. Friedrich-Wilhelm von Herrmann, 1984.

GA 46. *Zur Auslegung von Nietzsches II. Unzeitgemäßer Betrachtung "Vom Nutzen und Nachteil der Historie für das Leben"* (1938–9). Ed. Hans-Joachim Friedrich, 2003.

GA 47. *Nietzsches Lehre vom Willen zur Macht als Erkenntnis* (1939). Ed. Eberhard Hanser, 1989.

GA 48. *Nietzsche: Der europäische Nihilismus* (1940). Ed. Petra Jaeger, 1986.

GA 49. *Die Metaphysik des deutschen Idealismus. Zur erneuten Auslegung von Schelling: "Philosophische Untersuchungen über das Wesen der menschlichen Freiheit und die damit zusammenhängenden Gegenstände" (1809)* (1941). Ed. Günter Seubold, 1991, 2006 (2nd rev. ed.).

GA 50. *Nietzsches Metaphysik; Einleitung in die Philosophie – Denken und Dichten* (1941–2, 1944–5). Ed. Petra Jaeger, 1990, 2007 (2nd rev. ed.).

GA 51. *Grundbegriffe* (1941). Ed. Petra Jaeger, 1981, 1991 (rev. ed.).

GA 52. *Hölderlins Hymne "Andenken"* (1941–2). Ed. Curd Ochwadt, 1982.

GA 53. *Hölderlins Hymne "Der Ister"* (1942). Ed. Walter Biemel, 1984.

GA 54. *Parmenides* (1942–3). Ed. Manfred S. Frings, 1982.

GA 55. *Heraklit* (1943, 1944). Ed. Manfred S. Frings, 1979, 1987 (rev. ed.).

GA 56/57. *Zur Bestimmung der Philosophie* (1919). Ed. Bernd Heimbüchel, 1987, 1999 (rev., expanded ed.).

GA 60. *Phänomenologie des religiösen Lebens* (1918–21). Ed. Matthias Jung, Thomas Regehly, and Claudius Strube, 1995, 2011 (rev. ed.).

GA 61. *Phänomenologische Interpretationen zu Aristoteles. Einführung in die phänomenologische Forschung* (1921–2). Ed. Walter Bröcker und Käte Bröcker-Oltmanns, 1985, 1994 (rev. ed.).

GA 62. *Phänomenologische Interpretationen ausgewählter Abhandlungen des Aristoteles zu Ontologie und Logik.* (1922). Ed. Günther Neumann, 2005.

GA 63. *Ontologie. Hermeneutik der Faktizität* (1923). Ed. Käte Bröcker-Oltmanns, 1988.

GA 64. *Der Begriff der Zeit* (1924). Ed. Friedrich-Wilhelm von Herrmann, 2004.

GA 65. *Beiträge zur Philosophie (Vom Ereignis)* (1936–8). Ed. Friedrich-Wilhelm von Herrmann, 1989, 1994 (rev. ed.).

GA 66. *Besinnung* (1938–9). Ed. Friedrich-Wilhelm von Herrmann, 1997.

GA 67. *Metaphysik und Nihilismus* (1938–9, 1946–8). Ed. Hans-Joachim Friedrich, 1999.

GA 68. *Hegel* (1938–9, 1942). Ed. Ingrid Schüßler, 1993.

GA 69. *Die Geschichte des Seyns* (1938–40). Ed. Peter Trawny, 1998, 2012 (rev. ed.).

GA 70. *Über den Anfang* (1941). Ed. Paola-Ludovika Coriando, 2005.

GA 71. *Das Ereignis* (1941–2). Ed. Friedrich-Wilhelm von Herrmann, 2009.

GA 73.1 and 73.2. *Zum Ereignis-Denken* (1932–70s). Ed. Peter Trawny, 2013.

GA 74. *Zum Wesen der Sprache und Zur Frage nach der Kunst* (1935–60). Ed. Thomas Regehly, 2010.

GA 75. *Zu Hölderlin – Griechenlandreisen* (1939–70). Ed. Curd Ochwadt, 2000.

GA 76. *Leitgedanken zur Entstehung der Metaphysik, der neuzeitlichen Wissenschaft und der modernen Technik* (1935–55). Ed. Claudius Strube, 2009.

GA 77. *Feldweg-Gespräche* (1944–5). Ed. Ingrid Schüßler, 1995, 2007 (2nd rev. ed.).

GA 78. *Der Spruch des Anaximander* (1942). Ed. Ingeborg Schüßler, 2010.

GA 79. *Bremer und Freiburger Vorträge* (1949, 1957). Ed. Petra Jaeger, 1994.

GA 80.1 *Vorträge 1915 bis 1932.* Ed. Günther Neumann, 2016.

GA 80.2 *Vorträge. Teil 2: 1935–1967.* Ed. Günther Neumann, 2020.

GA 81. *Gedachtes.* Ed. Paola-Ludovika Coriando, 2007.

GA 82. *Zu eigenen Veröffentlichungen* (1936–ca. 1950). Ed. Friedrich-Wilhelm von Herrmann, 2018.

GA 83. *Seminare: Platon – Aristoteles – Augustinus* (1928–52). Ed. Mark Michalski, 2012.

GA 84.1. *Seminare: Kant – Leibniz – Schiller* (1931–6). Ed. Günther Neumann, 2013.

GA 86. *Seminare: Hegel – Schelling* (1927–57). Ed. Peter Trawny, 2011.

GA 87. *Nietzsche: Seminare 1937 und 1944.* Ed. Peter von Ruckteschell, 2004.

GA 88. *Seminare (Übungen) 1937/38 und 1941/42: 1. Die metaphysischen Grundstellungen des abendländischen Denkens; 2. Einübung in das philosophische Denken.* Ed. Alfred Denker, 2008.

GA 89. *Zollikoner Seminare* (1959–69). Ed. Peter Trawny, 2017.

GA 90. *Zu Ernst Jünger* (1934–54). Ed. Peter Trawny, 2004.

GA 94. *Überlegungen II-VI (Schwarze Hefte 1931–1938).* Ed. Peter Trawny, 2014.

GA 95. *Überlegungen VII-XI (Schwarze Hefte 1938–1939).* Ed. Peter Trawny, 2014.

GA 96. *Überlegungen XII-XV (Schwarze Hefte 1939–1941).* Ed. Peter Trawny, 2014.

GA 97. *Anmerkungen I-V (Schwarze Hefte 1942–1948).* Ed. Peter Trawny, 2015.

GA 98. *Anmerkungen VI-IX (Schwarze Hefte 1948/49–1951).* Ed. Peter Trawny, 2018.

GA 99. *Vier Hefte I und II (Schwarze Hefte 1947–1950).* Ed. Peter Trawny, 2019.

GA 100 *Vigiliae und Notturno (Schwarze Hefte 1952/53–1957).* Ed. Peter Trawny, 2020.

GA 101 *Winke I and II (Schwarze Hefte 1957–1959).* Ed. Peter Trawny, 2020.

Acknowledgments

Thinking is also *thanking*.

With abiding thanks for the sustaining love of my family.

My gratitude to students, friends, colleagues, and readers across the globe with whom I have had rich and productive discussions over the years.

Special thanks to my co-translator Marie Göbel; to Vladimír Leško, Beatrix Lepis, and the University of Košice in Slovakia; to Ian Alexander Moore; to Laureano Ralón; to Dean Kevin Spicer of Stonehill College; to David Ashton for his friendship across the pond; and to Len Husband for his kindness and steadfast support as editor of this University of Toronto Press series.

ೋನ್ಲ

Chapter 1 and the translation in Part II originally appeared in the journal *Epoché* in slightly different forms: 20:2 (Spring 2016); 12:2 (Spring 2008).

Chapter 3 is a modified version of a talk originally delivered in honor of Prof. William J. Richardson; a further modified version also appears as *"Sein*: After *Being and Time"* in *The Heidegger Lexicon*, ed. Mark Wrathall (Cambridge: Cambridge University Press, 2021).

Chapter 4 is a modified version of Chapter 30 in *After Heidegger?* ed. Gregory Fried and Richard Polt (London: Rowman and Littlefield, 2017).

Notes

Introduction

1 For more on Heidegger's notion of Being as "the Holy" (*das Heilige*) and as "the Source" (*der Ursprung*), see my "Introduction: Dwelling in Nearness to the Holy" in the collection of essays *Heidegger and the Holy*, ed. Richard Capobianco (London: Rowman and Littlefield, 2022).

PART I: STUDIES

1 Pindar's "Gold" and Heraclitus's "*Kosmos*" as Being Itself

1 All references to Heidegger's works are to the volumes in the *Gesamtausgabe* published by Vittorio Klostermann, Frankfurt am Main. (See also the section of this book "A Note on the Text and Heidegger's *Gesamtausgabe*.") The initial reference is in each case to (GA + volume number: page number), and all subsequent references in this chapter are simply to the page number. All translations are my own.

2 Richard Capobianco, *Heidegger's Way of Being* (Toronto: University of Toronto Press, 2014), 71. All translations of GA 55 herein this chapter and in *Heidegger's Way of Being* are my own, but for readers in English, a translation of GA 55 has recently been published: *Heraclitus: The Inception of Occidental Thinking. Logic: Heraclitus's Doctrine of the Logos*, trans. Julia Goesser Assaiante and S. Montgomery Ewegen (London: Bloomsbury, 2018).

3 *Pindar II, The Loeb Classical Library*, trans. William H. Race
   (Cambridge, MA: Harvard University Press), 174–5.
4 See also *Heidegger's Way of Being*, Chapter 2.
5 The relation of the word *kosmos* to Zeus and to Cretan political leaders
   is mentioned by Heidegger in the 1966 seminar at Le Thor, GA 15: 281.
6 Andrew Wyeth: *Looking In, Looking Out*, National Gallery of Art,
   Washington, DC, 4 May to 30 November 2014.

**2 In the *Black Notebooks*: The "Turn" Away from the Transcendental-
Phenomenological Positioning of *Being and Time* to the Thinking of
Being as *Physis* and *Aletheia***

1 Heidegger's *Schwarze Hefte* or *Black Notebooks* considered in this
   chapter have been collected in four volumes in his *Gesamtausgabe*,
   published by Vittorio Klostermann (Frankfurt am Main). These
   volumes are GA 94, 95, 96, and 97. In what follows, all translations
   are my own, and references are given as (GA + volume number:
   page number). A secondary source that offers thoughtful reflections
   on several of the issues in the *Black Notebooks* is: Wilhelm-Friedrich
   von Herrmann and Francesco Alfieri, *Martin Heidegger. Die Wahrheit
   über die Schwarzen Hefte* (Berlin: Duncker & Humblot, 2017).
2 GA 9: 332.
3 *Heidegger's Way of Being*, esp. Chapter 1, 11–13.
4 In GA 97, see also esp. 275, 281, 282, 286, 289, 367, 373, 392, 415, 421.
5 See *Heidegger's Way of Being*, Chapter 1; Chapter 3, 42, 45–7; Chapter 4,
   62–4; also Chapter 1 of this volume.

**3 Heidegger's Manifold Thinking of Being: In Honor of Prof. William
J. Richardson, S.J.**

1 All references are to the volumes of Heidegger's *Gesamtausgabe*
   (GA) published by Vittorio Klostermann, Frankfurt am Main.
   The references are given as follows: (GA + volume number: page
   number). All translations are my own.

4 Athena, Art, and Overcoming the Egoity of Our Age

1 *"Die Herkunft der Kunst und die Bestimmung des Denkens,"* in
   Denkerfahrungen: 1910–1976, ed. Hermann Heidegger (Frankfurt

am Main: Klostermann, 1983), 135–49. Recent English translation by Dimitrios Latsis, amended by Ullrich Haase: "The Provenance of Art and the Destination of Thought (1967)," *Journal of the British Society for Phenomenology*, 44:2 (2013), 119–28. References in the chapter follow this form: (English text/German text), but I have modified some English translations. The German text is now included in the recently published volume 80.2 of Heidegger's *Gesamtausgabe*, published by Vittorio Klostermann (Frankfurt am Main, 2020), but note that the page numbers of the German text given in this chapter refer to the 1983 version and not to the GA version.

2 GA 15: 331; *Four Seminars*, trans. Andrew Mitchell and François Raffoul (Bloomington: Indiana University Press, 2003), 38.

3 In my *Heidegger's Way of Being*, I point out the affinities of Heidegger's later thinking with American authors, such as Walt Whitman, e.e. cummings, and John Muir. With respect to Heidegger's "gods," one may also consider these lines from John Muir on being in the presence of Yosemite Falls at midnight: "How interesting does man become considered in his relations to the spirit of this rock and water! How significant does every atom of our world become amid the influences of those beings unseen, spiritual, angelic mountaineers that so throng these pure mansions of crystal foam and purple granite." From his letter to Mrs. Ezra S. Carr, 3 April 1871.

4 *Heidegger's Way of Being*, especially Chapter 2 "On Hölderlin on 'Nature's Gleaming.'" See also Chapter 1 of this volume.

5 Yet for Heidegger, Hölderlin's "Nature" (*die Natur*) does indeed name *physis* in the richest Greek way; see Chapter 2 of *Heidegger's Way of Being*.

6 GA 40: 17. In translation: *Introduction to Metaphysics*, trans. Gregory Fried and Richard Polt (New Haven, CT: Yale University Press, 2000), 15.

7 *Heidegger's Way of Being*, 64.

8 See especially his 1965 talk in honor of Ludwig Binswanger titled "On the Question Concerning the Determination of the Matter for Thinking," trans. Richard Capobianco and Marie Göbel in the journal *Epoché*, Volume 14, Issue 2 (Spring 2010), 213–23. See also Reflection 4 in Part III for more information on this talk.

9 See especially GA 55 *Heraklit*. See *Heidegger's Way of Being*, Chapters 5 and 6, as well as Chapter 1 of this volume.

10 For more on the matter of Being as "primordial truth," see *Heidegger's Way of Being*, esp. Chapter 4.

11 Heidegger studies needs to be open to consider how the best thinking in contemporary theoretical astrophysics (which is by no means mere "scientism" or "technicity") may dovetail Heidegger's later thinking of Being as "time-space" (*Zeit-Raum*) as *Physis* and *Aletheia*. We should consider, too, the remarkable nearness in spirit of the later Heidegger's theme of *Gelassenheit* ("releasement") with several of Albert Einstein's broader reflections: "A human being is part of the whole, called by us "Universe," a part limited in time and space. He experiences himself, his thoughts and feelings as something separated from the rest – a kind of optical delusion of his consciousness. This delusion is a kind of prison for us, restricting us to our personal desires and to affection for a few persons nearest to us. Our task must be to free ourselves from this prison by widening our circle of compassion to embrace all living creatures and the whole of nature in its beauty." From a letter Einstein wrote at age 70 (dated 4 March 1950) to Norman Salit (Einstein Archives, 61–226). See also a similarly worded letter by Einstein dated 12 February 1950 to Robert Marcus (Einstein Archives, 60–424/425/426). In document 60–425, he also states: "Not to nourish the illusion but to try to overcome it is the way for us to reach the attainable measure of inner peace." With thanks to Chaya Becker, Archivist, Albert Einstein Archives, The Hebrew University of Jerusalem.

12 For more on "the voice" of Being as the primordial *Logos*, see Chapter 6 of *Heidegger's Way of Being*.

13 See especially Chapter 1 of *Heidegger's Way of Being* and Chapter 1 of this volume. The later Heidegger "turned" away from his own transcendentally inclined statements about *das Sein* in *Being and Time* and in other places in the early work, for example, in *Being and Time*, section 43(c). For more on this, see Chapter 2.

14 GA 55: 171.

15 GA 55: 166.

5 *Mythos*, Being, and the Appropriation of a Religious Tradition

1 "*Logos* (Heraclitus, Fragment B 50)," in *Early Greek Thinking*, trans. David Farrell Krell and Frank A. Capuzzi (New York: Harper &

Row, 1984), 59–78. The essay was published in 1951, but Heidegger had discussed similar issues in a lecture course on Heraclitus in 1944; see *Heidegger's Way of Being*, Chapter 6. I follow the translation of Krell and Capuzzi in this section.

2 "*Logos*," references are to 72–4.

3 An important text in this regard is Heidegger's commentary on Aristotle's *Physics*. He finds fault with the "Hellenistic" and "Christian" translation of the ancient Greek word *aei* as "eternal." He writes, "*aei* means not only 'all the time' and 'incessant.' Rather, first of all it means 'at any given time.' *ho aei basileuon* = the one who is ruler at the time – not the 'eternal ruler.' With the word *aei* what one has in view is the notion of 'staying for a while,' specifically in the sense of presencing." See "On the Being and Conception of *physis* in Aristotle's *Physics* B, 1," in *Pathmarks*, ed. William McNeill (Cambridge: Cambridge University Press, 1998), 205–6.

4 GA 54, *Parmenides*, (Frankfurt am Main: Vittorio Klostermann, 1982), 162–7. All translations are my own, but the available published English translation of GA 54 is *Parmenides*, trans. André Schuwer and Richard Rojcewicz (Bloomington: Indiana University Press, 1992).

5 Here the German is *hereinblicken* and *scheinen*.

6 Heidegger qualifies this by adding that the *Gottsager* is only the "human being of the Greek experience."

7 GA 54: 164.

8 See also my "Introduction: Dwelling in Nearness to the Holy" in the volume of collected essays *Heidegger and the Holy*, ed. Richard Capobianco (London: Roman and Littlefield, 2022).

6 On Heidegger's Heraclitus Lectures: In Nearness of a Process Metaphysics?

1 Martin Heidegger, *Gesamtausgabe, Band 55: Heraklit: Der Anfang des abendländischen Denkens; Logik. Heraklits Lehre vom Logos*, ed. Manfred S. Frings (Frankfurt am Main: Vittorio Klostermann, 1979). All page numbers in parentheses refer to GA 55. All translations are my own, but as noted in Chapter 1, note 2, an English translation of GA 55 has recently been published.

2 See Chapters 5 and 6 of *Heidegger's Way of Being*.

7 The Path through Heidegger's Thought: Interview with Prof. Vladimír Leško for *FILOZOFIA*

1 This interview with Prof. Vladimír Leško was conducted in English and translated and published in Slovak in *FILOZOFIA* 5 (2017), 397–408. This version is updated and slightly modified from the original.

PART II: TRANSLATION

1 "Martin Heidegger's Thinking and Japanese Philosophy" by Kōichi Tsujimura and "Reply in Appreciation" by Martin Heidegger

1 Kōichi Tsujimura (1922–2010) was one of the most prominent figures of his generation in the so-called Kyōto School of thought in Japan. He was also widely regarded as the foremost Japanese interpreter and proponent of Martin Heidegger's thinking. From 1956 to 1958, Tsujimura studied with Heidegger in Freiburg, and in the subsequent years, he translated and commented upon a number of Heidegger's texts. Furthermore, in his own published work, he was much concerned with attempting to show the close connection between Heidegger's thinking and the tradition of reflection in Zen Buddhism and in the Kyōto School.

In 1969, the German town of Messkirch, Heidegger's birthplace, invited Tsujimura to give the keynote address at the town's celebration of Heidegger's 80th birthday. In the evening of September 26, Tsujimura delivered an engaging talk in German titled *Martin Heideggers Denken und die japanische Philosophie*. This address, along with other speeches and Heidegger's *Reply in Appreciation* (*Dankansprache*), was originally published by the town in the volume *Martin Heidegger – Ansprachen zum 80. Geburtstag am 26. September 1969 in Messkirch* (Messkirch: Heuberg-Druckerei F.G. Aker). Twenty years later, Tsujimura's text and a selection from Heidegger's reply (relating to Tsujimura's address) were published by Jan Thorbecke Verlag in a collection of writings titled *Japan und Heidegger* in commemoration of Heidegger's 100th birthday in 1989. Our translation of these two texts follows the Thorbecke Verlag edition (except for minor typographical errors that we have corrected), and we are grateful to the publisher for granting us the

translation rights. © Hartmut Buchner (Hg.). *Japan und Heidegger.*
Gedenkschrift der Stadt Messkirch zum hundertsten Geburtstag
Martin Heideggers. Herausgegeben im Auftrag der Stadt Messkirch
(Sigmaringen: Jan Thorbecke Verlag, 1989), 159–66.
Note that all the textual citations in the body of the texts are as
they appear in the Thorbecke edition and are not the translators'
interpolations. We have added corresponding notes indicated by
"Trans."

2 Trans.: The *Fukanzazengi* is Dōgen's earliest teaching statement
on Zen meditative practice (1227). This cornerstone text has been
translated into English many times, variously titled along the lines
of the *General Recommendations for the Practice of Zazen.*

3 Trans.: Cf. Martin Heidegger, *What is Called Thinking?* trans. J. Glenn
Gray (New York: Harper & Row Publishers, 1968), 37–44.

4 Trans.: Cf. Martin Heidegger, *Discourse on Thinking*, trans. John
M. Anderson and E. Hans Freund (New York: Harper & Row
Publishers, 1966), 66.

5 Trans.: The reference is to the fascicle "Plum Blossoms" (*Baika*)
written by Dōgen in 1243 as part of his life's work and masterwork
Treasury of the True Dharma Eye (*Shōbōgenzō*). Cf. "Plum Blossoms,"
in *Moon in a Dewdrop: Writings of Zen Master Dōgen*, ed. Kazuaki
Tanahashi (New York: North Point Press, 1995), 114–23.

6 Trans.: Cf. *What is Called Thinking?* 44.

7 *Aus Martin Heideggers Dankansprache*, in *Japan und Heidegger*, 166. See
initial note for complete information.

8 Trans.: This citation appears in the Thorbecke Verlag edition only.
Cf. Martin Heidegger, *Letter on Humanism* in *Pathmarks*, ed. William
McNeill (Cambridge: Cambridge University Press, 1998), 258.

9 Trans.: A mocking allusion to Marx's understanding of
"superstructure" (*Überbau*) is possible here.

PART III: REFLECTIONS AND IMPRESSIONS

4 Heidegger's "Clearing" Is Not Identical with the Human Being

1 For Heidegger's complete address in English translation by Richard
Capobianco and Marie Göbel, see the journal *Epoché*, Volume 14,
Issue 2 (Spring 2010), 213–23.

10 Heidegger and C.G. Jung on Wholeness as the Telos of the Human Being

1 See also my "Introduction: Dwelling in Nearness to the Holy" in the collection of essays *Heidegger and the Holy*, ed. Richard Capobianco (London: Rowman and Littlefield, 2022).

11 Heidegger and C.G. Jung on "Opposites"

1 *The Collected Works of C. G. Jung*, trans. R.F.C. Hull (Princeton, NJ: Princeton University Press). [CW, multiple volumes]; CW 6, para. 179.
2 CW 6, paras. 179, 181.
3 Heidegger, *Introduction to Metaphysics*, trans. Ralph Manheim (New Haven, CT: Yale University Press, 1959). [IM]; IM, 128, 131.
4 IM, 131.
5 IM, 133.
6 IM, 134.
7 Heidegger, *Nietzsche*, Vol. IV, *Nihilism*, trans. Frank A. Capuzzi (New York: Harper & Row, 1982). [N]; N, 222.
8 IM, 138.
9 Heidegger, "*Logos* (Heraclitus, Fragment B 50)," in Early Greek Thinking, trans. David Farrell Krell and Frank A. Capuzzi (New York: Harper & Row, 1984). [L]; L, 70.
10 L, 71.
11 L, 61.
12 Thomas Aquinas, *De Veritate*, q. 1, a. 12.
13 L, 70–1.
14 CW 14, paras. 759–75.

14 The Unspeakable Mystery of All Things

1 The priest's "chasuble" is the outermost vestment. It is interesting to consider whether Heidegger also had in mind here that the word "chasuble" is derived from the Latin word *casula*, which means a "small house." Is it possible that Heidegger refers to the chasuble because it brings us close to our proper "home" in relation to ultimate mystery?

2 Heidegger's reminder of "the ever *veiled* gift" surely calls to
   mind those words, "For now we see through a glass, darkly"
   (1 Corinthians 13:12).

15 A "Hermetic Saying" and the Hermetic Tradition

1 For the Latin text critical edition, see *Liber viginti quattuor
   philosophorum* (Corpus Christianorum. Continuatio Mediaevalis
   CXLIII A), ed. Francoise Hudry (Turnhout, Belgium: Brepols
   Publisher, 1997).

Index

New Studies in Phenomenology and Hermeneutics

General Editor: Kenneth Maly

Gail Stenstad, *Transformations: Thinking after Heidegger*
Parvis Emad, *On the Way to Heidegger's* Contributions to Philosophy
Bernhard Radloff, *Heidegger and the Question of National Socialism: Disclosure and Gestalt*
Kenneth Maly, *Heidegger's Possibility: Language, Emergence – Saying Be-ing*
Robert Mugerauer, *Heidegger and Homecoming: The Leitmotif in the Later Writings*
Graeme Nicholson, *Justifying Our Existence: An Essay in Applied Phenomenology*
Ladelle McWhorter and Gail Stenstad, eds., *Heidegger and the Earth: Essays in Environmental Philosophy, Second, Expanded Edition*
Richard Capobianco, *Engaging Heidegger*
Peter R. Costello, *Layers in Husserl's Phenomenology: On Meaning and Intersubjectivity*
Friedrich-Wilhelm von Herrmann, *Hermeneutics and Reflection: Heidegger and Husserl on the Concept of Phenomenology*. Translated by Kenneth Maly. Published in German as *Hermeneutik und Reflexion. Der Begriff der Phänomenologie bei Heidegger und Husserl*
Richard Capobianco, *Heidegger's Way of Being*
Janet Donohoe, *Husserl on Ethics and Intersubjectivity: From Static to Genetic Phenomenology*
Miles Groth, *Translating Heidegger*
Graeme Nicholson, *Heidegger on Truth: Its Essence and its Fate*
Kenneth Maly, *Five Ground-Breaking Moments in Heidegger's Thinking*
Richard Capobianco, *Heidegger's Being: The Shimmering Unfolding*